A Woman Of No Importance

A PLAY

BY
OSCAR WILDE

Table of Contents

THE PERSONS OF THE PLAY 4
THE SCENES OF THE PLAY 5
LONDON: HAYMARKET THEATRE 6
FIRST ACT 8
SECOND ACT 35
THIRD ACT 67
FOURTH ACT 92

TO
GLADYS
COUNTESS DE GREY

[MARCHIONESS OF RIPON]

THE PERSONS OF THE PLAY

LORD ILLINGWORTH

SIR JOHN PONTEFRACT

LORD ALFRED RUFFORD

MR. KELVIL, M.P.

THE VEN. ARCHDEACON DAUBENY, D.D.

GERALD ARBUTHNOT

FARQUHAR, Butler

FRANCIS, Footman

LADY HUNSTANTON

LADY CAROLINE PONTEFRACT

LADY STUTFIELD

MRS. ALLONBY

MISS HESTER WORSLEY

ALICE, Maid

MRS. ARBUTHNOT

THE SCENES OF THE PLAY

Act I. *The Terrace at Hunstanton Chase.*

Act II. *The Drawing-room at Hunstanton Chase.*

Act III. *The Hall at Hunstanton Chase.*

Act IV. *Sitting-room in Mrs. Arbuthnot's House at Wrockley.*

Time: *The Present.*

Place: *The Shires.*

The action of the play takes place within twenty-four hours.

LONDON: HAYMARKET THEATRE

Lessee and Manager: Mr. H Beerbohm Tree
April 19th, 1893

LORD ILLINGWORTH	*Mr. Tree.*
SIR JOHN PONTEFRACT	*Mr. E. Holman Clark.*
LORD ALFRED RUFFORD	*Mr. Ernest Lawford.*
MR. KELVIL, M.P.	*Mr. Charles Allan.*
THE VEN. ARCHDEACON DAUBENY, D.D.	*Mr. Kemble.*
GERALD ARBUTHNOT	*Mr. Terry.*
FARQUHAR (*Butler*)	*Mr. Hay.*
FRANCIS (*Footman*)	*Mr. Montague.*
LADY HUNSTANTON	*Miss Rose Leclercq.*
LADY CAROLINE PONTEFRACT	*Miss Le Thière.*
LADY STUTFIELD	*Miss Blanche Horlock.*
MRS. ALLONBY	*Mrs. Tree.*
MISS HESTER WORSLEY	*Miss Julia*

	Neilson.
ALICE (*Maid*)	*Miss Kelly.*
MRS. ARBUTHNOT	*Mrs. Bernard-Beere.*

FIRST ACT

SCENE

Lawn in front of the terrace at Hunstanton.

[SIR JOHN *and* LADY CAROLINE PONTEFRACT, MISS WORSLEY, *on chairs under large yew tree.*]

LADY CAROLINE. I believe this is the first English country house you have stayed at, Miss Worsley?

HESTER. Yes, Lady Caroline.

LADY CAROLINE. You have no country houses, I am told, in America?

HESTER. We have not many.

LADY CAROLINE. Have you any country? What we should call country?

HESTER. [*Smiling.*] We have the largest country in the world, Lady Caroline. They used to tell us at school that some of our states are as big as France and England put together.

LADY CAROLINE. Ah! you must find it very draughty, I should fancy. [*To* SIR JOHN.] John, you should have your muffler. What is the use of my always knitting mufflers for you if you won't wear them?

SIR JOHN. I am quite warm, Caroline, I assure you.

LADY CAROLINE. I think not, John. Well, you couldn't come to a more charming place than this, Miss Worsley, though the house is excessively damp, quite unpardonably damp, and dear Lady Hunstanton is sometimes a little lax about the people she asks down here. [*To* SIR JOHN.] Jane mixes too much. Lord Illingworth, of course, is a man of high distinction. It is a privilege to meet him. And that member of Parliament, Mr. Kettle—

SIR JOHN. Kelvil, my love, Kelvil.

LADY CAROLINE. He must be quite respectable. One has never heard his name before in the whole course of one's life, which speaks volumes for a man, nowadays. But Mrs. Allonby is hardly a very suitable person.

HESTER. I dislike Mrs. Allonby. I dislike her more than I can say.

LADY CAROLINE. I am not sure, Miss Worsley, that foreigners like yourself should cultivate likes or dislikes about the people they are invited to meet. Mrs. Allonby is very well born. She is a niece of Lord Brancaster's. It is said, of course, that she ran away twice before she was married. But you know how unfair people often are. I myself don't believe she ran away more than once.

HESTER. Mr. Arbuthnot is very charming.

LADY CAROLINE. Ah, yes! the young man who has a post in a bank. Lady Hunstanton is most kind in asking him here, and Lord Illingworth seems to have taken quite a fancy to him. I am not sure, however, that Jane is right in taking him out of his position. In my young days, Miss Worsley, one never met any one in society who worked for their living. It was not considered the thing.

HESTER. In America those are the people we respect most.

LADY CAROLINE. I have no doubt of it.

HESTER. Mr. Arbuthnot has a beautiful nature! He is so simple, so sincere. He has one of the most beautiful natures I have ever come across. It is a privilege to meet *him*.

LADY CAROLINE. It is not customary in England, Miss Worsley, for a young lady to speak with such enthusiasm of any person of the opposite sex. English women conceal their feelings till after they are married. They show them then.

HESTER. Do you, in England, allow no friendship to exist between a young man and a young girl?

[*Enter* LADY HUNSTANTON, *followed by Footman with shawls and a cushion.*]

LADY CAROLINE. We think it very inadvisable. Jane, I was just saying what a pleasant party you have asked us to meet. You have a wonderful power of selection. It is quite a gift.

LADY HUNSTANTON. Dear Caroline, how kind of you! I think we all do fit in very nicely together. And I hope our charming American visitor will carry back pleasant recollections of our English country life. [*To Footman.*] The cushion, there, Francis. And my shawl. The Shetland. Get the Shetland. [*Exit Footman for shawl.*]

[*Enter* GERALD ARBUTHNOT.]

GERALD. Lady Hunstanton, I have such good news to tell you. Lord Illingworth has just offered to make me his secretary.

LADY HUNSTANTON. His secretary? That is good news indeed, Gerald. It means a very brilliant future in store for you. Your dear mother will be delighted. I really must try and induce her to come up here to-night. Do you think she would, Gerald? I know how difficult it is to get her to go anywhere.

GERALD. Oh! I am sure she would, Lady Hunstanton, if she knew Lord Illingworth had made me such an offer.

[*Enter Footman with shawl.*]

LADY HUNSTANTON. I will write and tell her about it, and ask her to come up and meet him. [*To Footman.*] Just wait, Francis. [*Writes letter.*]

LADY CAROLINE. That is a very wonderful opening for so young a man as you are, Mr. Arbuthnot.

GERALD. It is indeed, Lady Caroline. I trust I shall be able to show myself worthy of it.

LADY CAROLINE. I trust so.

GERALD. [*To* HESTER.] *You* have not congratulated me yet, Miss Worsley.

HESTER. Are you very pleased about it?

GERALD. Of course I am. It means everything to me—things that were out of the reach of hope before may be within hope's reach now.

HESTER. Nothing should be out of the reach of hope. Life is a hope.

LADY HUNSTANTON. I fancy, Caroline, that Diplomacy is what Lord Illingworth is aiming at. I heard that he was offered Vienna. But that may not be true.

LADY CAROLINE. I don't think that England should be represented abroad by an unmarried man, Jane. It might lead to complications.

LADY HUNSTANTON. You are too nervous, Caroline. Believe me, you are too nervous. Besides, Lord Illingworth may marry any day. I was in hopes he would have married lady Kelso. But I believe he said her family was too large. Or was it her feet? I forget which. I regret it very much. She was made to be an ambassador's wife.

LADY CAROLINE. She certainly has a wonderful faculty of remembering people's names, and forgetting their faces.

LADY HUNSTANTON. Well, that is very natural, Caroline, is it not? [*To Footman.*] Tell Henry to wait for an answer. I have written a line to your dear mother, Gerald, to tell her your good news, and to say she really must come to dinner.

[*Exit Footman.*]

GERALD. That is awfully kind of you, Lady Hunstanton. [*To* HESTER.] Will you come for a stroll, Miss Worsley?

HESTER. With pleasure. [*Exit with* GERALD.]

LADY HUNSTANTON. I am very much gratified at Gerald Arbuthnot's good fortune. He is quite a *protégé* of mine. And I am particularly pleased that Lord Illingworth should have made the offer of his own accord without my suggesting anything. Nobody likes to be asked favours. I remember poor Charlotte Pagden making herself quite unpopular one season, because she had a French governess she wanted to recommend to every one.

LADY CAROLINE. I saw the governess, Jane. Lady Pagden sent her to me. It was before Eleanor came out. She was far too good-looking to be in any respectable household. I don't wonder Lady Pagden was so anxious to get rid of her.

LADY HUNSTANTON. Ah, that explains it.

LADY CAROLINE. John, the grass is too damp for you. You had better go and put on your overshoes at once.

SIR JOHN. I am quite comfortable, Caroline, I assure you.

LADY CAROLINE. You must allow me to be the best judge of that, John. Pray do as I tell you.

[SIR JOHN *gets up and goes off.*]

LADY HUNSTANTON. You spoil him, Caroline, you do indeed!

[*Enter* MRS. ALLONBY *and* LADY STUTFIELD.]

[*To* MRS. ALLONBY.] Well, dear, I hope you like the park. It is said to be well timbered.

MRS. ALLONBY. The trees are wonderful, Lady Hunstanton.

LADY STUTFIELD. Quite, quite wonderful.

MRS. ALLONBY. But somehow, I feel sure that if I lived in the country for six months, I should become so unsophisticated that no one would take the slightest notice of me.

LADY HUNSTANTON. I assure you, dear, that the country has not that effect at all. Why, it was from Melthorpe, which is only two miles from here, that Lady Belton eloped with Lord Fethersdale. I remember the occurrence perfectly. Poor Lord Belton died three days afterwards of joy, or gout. I forget which. We had a large party staying here at the time, so we were all very much interested in the whole affair.

MRS. ALLONBY. I think to elope is cowardly. It's running away from danger. And danger has become so rare in modern life.

LADY CAROLINE. As far as I can make out, the young women of the present day seem to make it the sole object of their lives to be always playing with fire.

MRS. ALLONBY. The one advantage of playing with fire, Lady Caroline, is that one never gets even singed. It is the people who don't know how to play with it who get burned up.

LADY STUTFIELD. Yes; I see that. It is very, very helpful.

LADY HUNSTANTON. I don't know how the world would get on with such a theory as that, dear Mrs. Allonby.

LADY STUTFIELD. Ah! The world was made for men and not for women.

MRS. ALLONBY. Oh, don't say that, Lady Stutfield. We have a much better time than they have. There are far more things forbidden to us than are forbidden to them.

LADY STUTFIELD. Yes; that is quite, quite true. I had not thought of that.

[*Enter* SIR JOHN *and* MR. KELVIL.]

LADY HUNSTANTON. Well, Mr. Kelvil, have you got through your work?

KELVIL. I have finished my writing for the day, Lady Hunstanton. It has been an arduous task. The demands on the time of a public man are very heavy nowadays, very heavy indeed. And I don't think they meet with adequate recognition.

LADY CAROLINE. John, have you got your overshoes on?

SIR JOHN. Yes, my love.

LADY CAROLINE. I think you had better come over here, John. It is more sheltered.

SIR JOHN. I am quite comfortable, Caroline.

LADY CAROLINE. I think not, John. You had better sit beside me. [SIR JOHN *rises and goes across*.]

LADY STUTFIELD. And what have you been writing about this morning, Mr. Kelvil?

KELVIL. On the usual subject, Lady Stutfield. On Purity.

LADY STUTFIELD. That must be such a very, very interesting thing to write about.

KELVIL. It is the one subject of really national importance, nowadays, Lady Stutfield. I purpose addressing my constituents on the question before Parliament meets. I find that the poorer classes of this country display a marked desire for a higher ethical standard.

LADY STUTFIELD. How quite, quite nice of them.

LADY CAROLINE. Are you in favour of women taking part in politics, Mr. Kettle?

SIR JOHN. Kelvil, my love, Kelvil.

KELVIL. The growing influence of women is the one reassuring thing in our political life, Lady Caroline. Women are always on the side of morality, public and private.

LADY STUTFIELD. It is so very, very gratifying to hear you say that.

LADY HUNSTANTON. Ah, yes!—the moral qualities in women—that is the important thing. I am afraid, Caroline, that dear Lord Illingworth doesn't value the moral qualities in women as much as he should.

[*Enter* LORD ILLINGWORTH.]

LADY STUTFIELD. The world says that Lord Illingworth is very, very wicked.

LORD ILLINGWORTH. But what world says that, Lady Stutfield? It must be the next world. This world and I are on excellent terms. [*Sits down beside* MRS. ALLONBY.]

LADY STUTFIELD. Every one *I* know says you are very, very wicked.

LORD ILLINGWORTH. It is perfectly monstrous the way people go about, nowadays, saying things against one behind one's back that are absolutely and entirely true.

LADY HUNSTANTON. Dear Lord Illingworth is quite hopeless, Lady Stutfield. I have given up trying to reform him. It would take a Public Company with a Board of Directors and a paid Secretary to do that. But you have the secretary already, Lord Illingworth, haven't you? Gerald Arbuthnot has told us of his good fortune; it is really most kind of you.

LORD ILLINGWORTH. Oh, don't say that, Lady Hunstanton. Kind is a dreadful word. I took a great fancy to young Arbuthnot the moment I met him, and he'll be of considerable use to me in something I am foolish enough to think of doing.

LADY HUNSTANTON. He is an admirable young man. And his mother is one of my dearest friends. He has just gone for a walk with our pretty American. She is very pretty, is she not?

LADY CAROLINE. Far too pretty. These American girls carry off all the good matches. Why can't they stay in their own country? They are always telling us it is the Paradise of women.

LORD ILLINGWORTH. It is, Lady Caroline. That is why, like Eve, they are so extremely anxious to get out of it.

LADY CAROLINE. Who are Miss Worsley's parents?

LORD ILLINGWORTH. American women are wonderfully clever in concealing their parents.

LADY HUNSTANTON. My dear Lord Illingworth, what do you mean? Miss Worsley, Caroline, is an orphan. Her father was a very wealthy millionaire or philanthropist, or both, I believe, who entertained my son quite hospitably, when he visited Boston. I don't know how he made his money, originally.

KELVIL. I fancy in American dry goods.

LADY HUNSTANTON. What are American dry goods?

LORD ILLINGWORTH. American novels.

LADY HUNSTANTON. How very singular! . . . Well, from whatever source her large fortune came, I have a great esteem for Miss Worsley. She dresses exceedingly well. All Americans do dress well. They get their clothes in Paris.

MRS. ALLONBY. They say, Lady Hunstanton, that when good Americans die they go to Paris.

LADY HUNSTANTON. Indeed? And when bad Americans die, where do they go to?

LORD ILLINGWORTH. Oh, they go to America.

KELVIL. I am afraid you don't appreciate America, Lord Illingworth. It is a very remarkable country, especially considering its youth.

LORD ILLINGWORTH. The youth of America is their oldest tradition. It has been going on now for three hundred years. To hear them talk one would imagine they were in their first childhood. As far as civilisation goes they are in their second.

KELVIL. There is undoubtedly a great deal of corruption in American politics. I suppose you allude to that?

LORD ILLINGWORTH. I wonder.

LADY HUNSTANTON. Politics are in a sad way everywhere, I am told. They certainly are in England. Dear Mr. Cardew is ruining the country. I wonder Mrs. Cardew allows him. I am sure, Lord Illingworth, you don't think that uneducated people should be allowed to have votes?

LORD ILLINGWORTH. I think they are the only people who should.

KELVIL. Do you take no side then in modern politics, Lord Illingworth?

LORD ILLINGWORTH. One should never take sides in anything, Mr. Kelvil. Taking sides is the beginning of sincerity, and earnestness follows shortly afterwards, and the human being becomes a bore. However, the House of Commons really does very little harm. You can't make people good by Act of Parliament,—that is something.

KELVIL. You cannot deny that the House of Commons has always shown great sympathy with the sufferings of the poor.

LORD ILLINGWORTH. That is its special vice. That is the special vice of the age. One should sympathise with the joy, the beauty, the colour of life. The less said about life's sores the better, Mr. Kelvil.

KELVIL. Still our East End is a very important problem.

LORD ILLINGWORTH. Quite so. It is the problem of slavery. And we are trying to solve it by amusing the slaves.

LADY HUNSTANTON. Certainly, a great deal may be done by means of cheap entertainments, as you say, Lord Illingworth. Dear Dr. Daubeny, our rector here, provides, with the assistance of his curates, really admirable recreations for the poor during the winter. And much good may be done by means of a magic lantern, or a missionary, or some popular amusement of that kind.

LADY CAROLINE. I am not at all in favour of amusements for the poor, Jane. Blankets and coals are sufficient. There is too much love of pleasure amongst the upper classes as it is. Health is what we want in modern life. The tone is not healthy, not healthy at all.

KELVIL. You are quite right, Lady Caroline.

LADY CAROLINE. I believe I am usually right.

MRS. ALLONBY. Horrid word 'health.'

LORD ILLINGWORTH. Silliest word in our language, and one knows so well the popular idea of health. The English country gentleman galloping after a fox—the unspeakable in full pursuit of the uneatable.

KELVIL. May I ask, Lord Illingworth, if you regard the House of Lords as a better institution than the House of Commons?

LORD ILLINGWORTH. A much better institution, of course. We in the House of Lords are never in touch with public opinion. That makes us a civilised body.

KELVIL. Are you serious in putting forward such a view?

LORD ILLINGWORTH. Quite serious, Mr. Kelvil. [*To* MRS. ALLONBY.] Vulgar habit that is people have nowadays of asking one, after one has given them an idea, whether one is serious or not. Nothing is serious except passion. The intellect is not a serious thing, and never has been. It is an instrument on which one plays, that is all. The only serious form of intellect I know is the British intellect. And on the British intellect the illiterates play the drum.

LADY HUNSTANTON. What are you saying, Lord Illingworth, about the drum?

LORD ILLINGWORTH. I was merely talking to Mrs. Allonby about the leading articles in the London newspapers.

LADY HUNSTANTON. But do you believe all that is written in the newspapers?

LORD ILLINGWORTH. I do. Nowadays it is only the unreadable that occurs. [*Rises with* MRS. ALLONBY.]

LADY HUNSTANTON. Are you going, Mrs. Allonby?

MRS. ALLONBY. Just as far as the conservatory. Lord Illingworth told me this morning that there was an orchid there as beautiful as the seven deadly sins.

LADY HUNSTANTON. My dear, I hope there is nothing of the kind. I will certainly speak to the gardener.

[*Exit* MRS. ALLONBY *and* LORD ILLINGWORTH.]

LADY CAROLINE. Remarkable type, Mrs. Allonby.

LADY HUNSTANTON. She lets her clever tongue run away with her sometimes.

LADY CAROLINE. Is that the only thing, Jane, Mrs. Allonby allows to run away with her?

LADY HUNSTANTON. I hope so, Caroline, I am sure.

[*Enter* LORD ALFRED.]

Dear Lord Alfred, do join us. [LORD ALFRED *sits down beside* LADY STUTFIELD.]

LADY CAROLINE. You believe good of every one, Jane. It is a great fault.

LADY STUTFIELD. Do you really, really think, Lady Caroline, that one should believe evil of every one?

LADY CAROLINE. I think it is much safer to do so, Lady Stutfield. Until, of course, people are found out to be good. But that requires a great deal of investigation nowadays.

LADY STUTFIELD. But there is so much unkind scandal in modern life.

LADY CAROLINE. Lord Illingworth remarked to me last night at dinner that the basis of every scandal is an absolutely immoral certainty.

KELVIL. Lord Illingworth is, of course, a very brilliant man, but he seems to me to be lacking in that fine faith in the nobility and purity of life which is so important in this century.

LADY STUTFIELD. Yes, quite, quite important, is it not?

KELVIL. He gives me the impression of a man who does not appreciate the beauty of our English home-life. I would say that he was tainted with foreign ideas on the subject.

LADY STUTFIELD. There is nothing, nothing like the beauty of home-life, is there?

KELVIL. It is the mainstay of our moral system in England, Lady Stutfield. Without it we would become like our neighbours.

LADY STUTFIELD. That would be so, so sad, would it not?

KELVIL. I am afraid, too, that Lord Illingworth regards woman simply as a toy. Now, I have never regarded woman as a toy. Woman is the intellectual helpmeet of man in public as in private life. Without her we should forget the true ideals. [*Sits down beside* LADY STUTFIELD.]

LADY STUTFIELD. I am so very, very glad to hear you say that.

LADY CAROLINE. You a married man, Mr. Kettle?

SIR JOHN. Kelvil, dear, Kelvil.

KELVIL. I am married, Lady Caroline.

LADY CAROLINE. Family?

KELVIL. Yes.

LADY CAROLINE. How many?

KELVIL. Eight.

[LADY STUTFIELD *turns her attention to* LORD ALFRED.]

LADY CAROLINE. Mrs. Kettle and the children are, I suppose, at the seaside? [SIR JOHN *shrugs his shoulders.*]

KELVIL. My wife is at the seaside with the children, Lady Caroline.

LADY CAROLINE. You will join them later on, no doubt?

KELVIL. If my public engagements permit me.

LADY CAROLINE. Your public life must be a great source of gratification to Mrs. Kettle.

SIR JOHN. Kelvil, my love, Kelvil.

LADY STUTFIELD. [*To* LORD ALFRED.] How very, very charming those gold-tipped cigarettes of yours are, Lord Alfred.

LORD ALFRED. They are awfully expensive. I can only afford them when I'm in debt.

LADY STUTFIELD. It must be terribly, terribly distressing to be in debt.

LORD ALFRED. One must have some occupation nowadays. If I hadn't my debts I shouldn't have anything to think about. All the chaps I know are in debt.

LADY STUTFIELD. But don't the people to whom you owe the money give you a great, great deal of annoyance?

[*Enter Footman.*]

LORD ALFRED. Oh, no, they write; I don't.

LADY STUTFIELD. How very, very strange.

LADY HUNSTANTON. Ah, here is a letter, Caroline, from dear Mrs. Arbuthnot. She won't dine. I am so sorry. But she will come in the evening. I am very pleased indeed. She is one of the sweetest of women. Writes a beautiful hand, too, so large, so firm. [*Hands letter to* LADY CAROLINE.]

LADY CAROLINE. [*Looking at it.*] A little lacking in femininity, Jane. Femininity is the quality I admire most in women.

LADY HUNSTANTON. [*Taking back letter and leaving it on table.*] Oh! she is very feminine, Caroline, and so good too. You should hear what the Archdeacon says of her. He regards her as his right hand in the parish. [*Footman speaks to her.*] In the Yellow Drawing-room. Shall we all go in? Lady Stutfield, shall we go in to tea?

LADY STUTFIELD. With pleasure, Lady Hunstanton. [*They rise and proceed to go off.* SIR JOHN *offers to carry* LADY STUTFIELD'S *cloak.*]

LADY CAROLINE. John! If you would allow your nephew to look after Lady Stutfield's cloak, you might help me with my workbasket.

[*Enter* LORD ILLINGWORTH *and* MRS. ALLONBY.]

SIR JOHN. Certainly, my love. [*Exeunt.*]

MRS. ALLONBY. Curious thing, plain women are always jealous of their husbands, beautiful women never are!

LORD ILLINGWORTH. Beautiful women never have time. They are always so occupied in being jealous of other people's husbands.

MRS. ALLONBY. I should have thought Lady Caroline would have grown tired of conjugal anxiety by this time! Sir John is her fourth!

LORD ILLINGWORTH. So much marriage is certainly not becoming. Twenty years of romance make a woman look like a ruin; but twenty years of marriage make her something like a public building.

MRS. ALLONBY. Twenty years of romance! Is there such a thing?

LORD ILLINGWORTH. Not in our day. Women have become too brilliant. Nothing spoils a romance so much as a sense of humour in the woman.

MRS. ALLONBY. Or the want of it in the man.

LORD ILLINGWORTH. You are quite right. In a Temple every one should be serious, except the thing that is worshipped.

MRS. ALLONBY. And that should be man?

LORD ILLINGWORTH. Women kneel so gracefully; men don't.

MRS. ALLONBY. You are thinking of Lady Stutfield!

LORD ILLINGWORTH. I assure you I have not thought of Lady Stutfield for the last quarter of an hour.

MRS. ALLONBY. Is she such a mystery?

LORD ILLINGWORTH. She is more than a mystery—she is a mood.

MRS. ALLONBY. Moods don't last.

LORD ILLINGWORTH. It is their chief charm.

[*Enter* HESTER *and* GERALD.]

GERALD. Lord Illingworth, every one has been congratulating me, Lady Hunstanton and Lady Caroline, and . . . every one. I hope I shall make a good secretary.

LORD ILLINGWORTH. You will be the pattern secretary, Gerald. [*Talks to him.*]

MRS. ALLONBY. You enjoy country life, Miss Worsley?

HESTER. Very much indeed.

MRS. ALLONBY. Don't find yourself longing for a London dinner-party?

HESTER. I dislike London dinner-parties.

MRS. ALLONBY. I adore them. The clever people never listen, and the stupid people never talk.

HESTER. I think the stupid people talk a great deal.

MRS. ALLONBY. Ah, I never listen!

LORD ILLINGWORTH. My dear boy, if I didn't like you I wouldn't have made you the offer. It is because I like you so much that I want to have you with me.

[*Exit* HESTER *with* GERALD.]

Charming fellow, Gerald Arbuthnot!

MRS. ALLONBY. He is very nice; very nice indeed. But I can't stand the American young lady.

LORD ILLINGWORTH. Why?

MRS. ALLONBY. She told me yesterday, and in quite a loud voice too, that she was only eighteen. It was most annoying.

LORD ILLINGWORTH. One should never trust a woman who tells one her real age. A woman who would tell one that, would tell one anything.

MRS. ALLONBY. She is a Puritan besides—

LORD ILLINGWORTH. Ah, that is inexcusable. I don't mind plain women being Puritans. It is the only excuse they have for being plain. But she is decidedly pretty. I admire her immensely. [*Looks steadfastly at* MRS. ALLONBY.]

MRS. ALLONBY. What a thoroughly bad man you must be!

LORD ILLINGWORTH. What do you call a bad man?

MRS. ALLONBY. The sort of man who admires innocence.

LORD ILLINGWORTH. And a bad woman?

MRS. ALLONBY. Oh! the sort of woman a man never gets tired of.

LORD ILLINGWORTH. You are severe—on yourself.

MRS. ALLONBY. Define us as a sex.

LORD ILLINGWORTH. Sphinxes without secrets.

MRS. ALLONBY. Does that include the Puritan women?

LORD ILLINGWORTH. Do you know, I don't believe in the existence of Puritan women? I don't think there is a woman in the world who would not be a little flattered if one made love to her. It is that which makes women so irresistibly adorable.

MRS. ALLONBY. You think there is no woman in the world who would object to being kissed?

LORD ILLINGWORTH. Very few.

MRS. ALLONBY. Miss Worsley would not let you kiss her.

LORD ILLINGWORTH. Are you sure?

MRS. ALLONBY. Quite.

LORD ILLINGWORTH. What do you think she'd do if I kissed her?

MRS. ALLONBY. Either marry you, or strike you across the face with her glove. What would you do if she struck you across the face with her glove?

LORD ILLINGWORTH. Fall in love with her, probably.

MRS. ALLONBY. Then it is lucky you are not going to kiss her!

LORD ILLINGWORTH. Is that a challenge?

MRS. ALLONBY. It is an arrow shot into the air.

LORD ILLINGWORTH. Don't you know that I always succeed in whatever I try?

MRS. ALLONBY. I am sorry to hear it. We women adore failures. They lean on us.

LORD ILLINGWORTH. You worship successes. You cling to them.

MRS. ALLONBY. We are the laurels to hide their baldness.

LORD ILLINGWORTH. And they need you always, except at the moment of triumph.

MRS. ALLONBY. They are uninteresting then.

LORD ILLINGWORTH. How tantalising you are! [*A pause.*]

MRS. ALLONBY. Lord Illingworth, there is one thing I shall always like you for.

LORD ILLINGWORTH. Only one thing? And I have so many bad qualities.

MRS. ALLONBY. Ah, don't be too conceited about them. You may lose them as you grow old.

LORD ILLINGWORTH. I never intend to grow old. The soul is born old but grows young. That is the comedy of life.

MRS. ALLONBY. And the body is born young and grows old. That is life's tragedy.

LORD ILLINGWORTH. Its comedy also, sometimes. But what is the mysterious reason why you will always like me?

MRS. ALLONBY. It is that you have never made love to me.

LORD ILLINGWORTH. I have never done anything else.

MRS. ALLONBY. Really? I have not noticed it.

LORD ILLINGWORTH. How fortunate! It might have been a tragedy for both of us.

MRS. ALLONBY. We should each have survived.

LORD ILLINGWORTH. One can survive everything nowadays, except death, and live down anything except a good reputation.

MRS. ALLONBY. Have you tried a good reputation?

LORD ILLINGWORTH. It is one of the many annoyances to which I have never been subjected.

MRS. ALLONBY. It may come.

LORD ILLINGWORTH. Why do you threaten me?

MRS. ALLONBY. I will tell you when you have kissed the Puritan.

[*Enter Footman.*]

FRANCIS. Tea is served in the Yellow Drawing-room, my lord.

LORD ILLINGWORTH. Tell her ladyship we are coming in.

FRANCIS. Yes, my lord.

[*Exit.*]

LORD ILLINGWORTH. Shall we go in to tea?

MRS. ALLONBY. Do you like such simple pleasures?

LORD ILLINGWORTH. I adore simple pleasures. They are the last refuge of the complex. But, if you wish, let us stay here. Yes, let us stay here. The Book of Life begins with a man and a woman in a garden.

MRS. ALLONBY. It ends with Revelations.

LORD ILLINGWORTH. You fence divinely. But the button has come of your foil.

MRS. ALLONBY. I have still the mask.

LORD ILLINGWORTH. It makes your eyes lovelier.

MRS. ALLONBY. Thank you. Come.

LORD ILLINGWORTH. [*Sees* MRS. ARBUTHNOT'S *letter on table, and takes it up and looks at envelope.*] What a curious handwriting! It reminds me of the handwriting of a woman I used to know years ago.

MRS. ALLONBY. Who?

LORD ILLINGWORTH. Oh! no one. No one in particular. A woman of no importance. [*Throws letter down, and passes up the steps of the terrace with* MRS. ALLONBY. *They smile at each other.*]

ACT DROP.

SECOND ACT

SCENE

Drawing-room at Hunstanton, after dinner, lamps lit. Door L.C. *Door* R.C.

[*Ladies seated on sofas.*]

MRS. ALLONBY. What a comfort it is to have got rid of the men for a little!

LADY STUTFIELD. Yes; men persecute us dreadfully, don't they?

MRS. ALLONBY. Persecute us? I wish they did.

LADY HUNSTANTON. My dear!

MRS. ALLONBY. The annoying thing is that the wretches can be perfectly happy without us. That is why I think it is every woman's duty never to leave them alone for a single moment, except during this short breathing space after dinner; without which I believe we poor women would be absolutely worn to shadows.

[*Enter Servants with coffee.*]

LADY HUNSTANTON. Worn to shadows, dear?

MRS. ALLONBY. Yes, Lady Hunstanton. It is such a strain keeping men up to the mark. They are always trying to escape from us.

LADY STUTFIELD. It seems to me that it is we who are always trying to escape from them. Men are so very, very heartless. They know their power and use it.

LADY CAROLINE. [*Takes coffee from Servant.*] What stuff and nonsense all this about men is! The thing to do is to keep men in their proper place.

MRS. ALLONBY. But what is their proper place, Lady Caroline?

LADY CAROLINE. Looking after their wives, Mrs. Allonby.

MRS. ALLONBY. [*Takes coffee from Servant.*] Really? And if they're not married?

LADY CAROLINE. If they are not married, they should be looking after a wife. It's perfectly scandalous the amount of bachelors who are going about society. There should be a law passed to compel them all to marry within twelve months.

LADY STUTFIELD. [*Refuses coffee.*] But if they're in love with some one who, perhaps, is tied to another?

LADY CAROLINE. In that case, Lady Stutfield, they should be married off in a week to some plain respectable girl, in order to teach them not to meddle with other people's property.

MRS. ALLONBY. I don't think that we should ever be spoken of as other people's property. All men are married women's property. That is the only true definition of what married women's property really is. But we don't belong to any one.

LADY STUTFIELD. Oh, I am so very, very glad to hear you say so.

LADY HUNSTANTON. But do you really think, dear Caroline, that legislation would improve matters in any way? I am told that, nowadays, all the married men live like bachelors, and all the bachelors like married men.

MRS. ALLONBY. I certainly never know one from the other.

LADY STUTFIELD. Oh, I think one can always know at once whether a man has home claims upon his life or not. I have noticed a very, very sad expression in the eyes of so many married men.

MRS. ALLONBY. Ah, all that I have noticed is that they are horribly tedious when they are good husbands, and abominably conceited when they are not.

LADY HUNSTANTON. Well, I suppose the type of husband has completely changed since my young days, but I'm bound to state that poor dear Hunstanton was the most delightful of creatures, and as good as gold.

MRS. ALLONBY. Ah, my husband is a sort of promissory note; I'm tired of meeting him.

LADY CAROLINE. But you renew him from time to time, don't you?

MRS. ALLONBY. Oh no, Lady Caroline. I have only had one husband as yet. I suppose you look upon me as quite an amateur.

LADY CAROLINE. With your views on life I wonder you married at all.

MRS. ALLONBY. So do I.

LADY HUNSTANTON. My dear child, I believe you are really very happy in your married life, but that you like to hide your happiness from others.

MRS. ALLONBY. I assure you I was horribly deceived in Ernest.

LADY HUNSTANTON. Oh, I hope not, dear. I knew his mother quite well. She was a Stratton, Caroline, one of Lord Crowland's daughters.

LADY CAROLINE. Victoria Stratton? I remember her perfectly. A silly fair-haired woman with no chin.

MRS. ALLONBY. Ah, Ernest has a chin. He has a very strong chin, a square chin. Ernest's chin is far too square.

LADY STUTFIELD. But do you really think a man's chin can be too square? I think a man should look very, very strong, and that his chin should be quite, quite square.

MRS. ALLONBY. Then you should certainly know Ernest, Lady Stutfield. It is only fair to tell you beforehand he has got no conversation at all.

LADY STUTFIELD. I adore silent men.

MRS. ALLONBY. Oh, Ernest isn't silent. He talks the whole time. But he has got no conversation. What he talks about I don't know. I haven't listened to him for years.

LADY STUTFIELD. Have you never forgiven him then? How sad that seems! But all life is very, very sad, is it not?

MRS. ALLONBY. Life, Lady Stutfield, is simply a *mauvais quart d'heure* made up of exquisite moments.

LADY STUTFIELD. Yes, there are moments, certainly. But was it something very, very wrong that Mr. Allonby did? Did he become angry with you, and say anything that was unkind or true?

MRS. ALLONBY. Oh dear, no. Ernest is invariably calm. That is one of the reasons he always gets on my nerves. Nothing is so aggravating as calmness. There is something positively brutal about the good temper of most modern men. I wonder we women stand it as well as we do.

LADY STUTFIELD. Yes; men's good temper shows they are not so sensitive as we are, not so finely strung. It makes a great barrier often between husband and wife, does it not? But I would so much like to know what was the wrong thing Mr. Allonby did.

MRS. ALLONBY. Well, I will tell you, if you solemnly promise to tell everybody else.

LADY STUTFIELD. Thank you, thank you. I will make a point of repeating it.

MRS. ALLONBY. When Ernest and I were engaged, he swore to me positively on his knees that he had never loved any one before in the whole course of his life. I was very young at the time, so I didn't believe him, I needn't tell you. Unfortunately, however, I made no enquiries of any kind till after I had been actually married four or five months. I found out then that what he had told me was perfectly true. And that sort of thing makes a man so absolutely uninteresting.

LADY HUNSTANTON. My dear!

MRS. ALLONBY. Men always want to be a woman's first love. That is their clumsy vanity. We women have a more subtle instinct about things. What we like is to be a man's last romance.

LADY STUTFIELD. I see what you mean. It's very, very beautiful.

LADY HUNSTANTON. My dear child, you don't mean to tell me that you won't forgive your husband because he never loved any one else? Did you ever hear such a thing, Caroline? I am quite surprised.

LADY CAROLINE. Oh, women have become so highly educated, Jane, that nothing should surprise us nowadays, except happy marriages. They apparently are getting remarkably rare.

MRS. ALLONBY. Oh, they're quite out of date.

LADY STUTFIELD. Except amongst the middle classes, I have been told.

MRS. ALLONBY. How like the middle classes!

LADY STUTFIELD. Yes—is it not?—very, very like them.

LADY CAROLINE. If what you tell us about the middle classes is true, Lady Stutfield, it redounds greatly to their credit. It is much to be regretted that in our rank of life the wife should be so persistently frivolous, under the impression apparently that it is the proper thing to be. It is to that I attribute the unhappiness of so many marriages we all know of in society.

MRS. ALLONBY. Do you know, Lady Caroline, I don't think the frivolity of the wife has ever anything to do with it. More marriages are ruined nowadays by the common sense of the husband than by anything else. How can a woman be expected to be happy with a man who insists on treating her as if she were a perfectly rational being?

LADY HUNSTANTON. My dear!

MRS. ALLONBY. Man, poor, awkward, reliable, necessary man belongs to a sex that has been rational for millions and millions of years. He can't help himself. It is in his race. The History of Woman is very different. We have always been picturesque protests against the mere existence of common sense. We saw its dangers from the first.

LADY STUTFIELD. Yes, the common sense of husbands is certainly most, most trying. Do tell me your conception of the Ideal Husband. I think it would be so very, very helpful.

MRS. ALLONBY. The Ideal Husband? There couldn't be such a thing. The institution is wrong.

LADY STUTFIELD. The Ideal Man, then, in his relations to *us*.

LADY CAROLINE. He would probably be extremely realistic.

Mrs. Caroline. The Ideal Man! Oh, the Ideal Man should talk to us as if we were goddesses, and treat us as if we were children. He should refuse all our serious requests, and gratify every one of our whims. He should encourage us to have caprices, and forbid us to have missions. He should always say much more than he means, and always mean much more than he says.

Lady Hunstanton. But how could he do both, dear?

Mrs. Allonby. He should never run down other pretty women. That would show he had no taste, or make one suspect that he had too much. No; he should be nice about them all, but say that somehow they don't attract him.

Lady Stutfield. Yes, that is always very, very pleasant to hear about other women.

Mrs. Allonby. If we ask him a question about anything, he should give us an answer all about ourselves. He should invariably praise us for whatever qualities he knows we haven't got. But he should be pitiless, quite pitiless, in reproaching us for the virtues that we have never dreamed of possessing. He should never believe that we know the use of useful things. That would be unforgiveable. But he should shower on us everything we don't want.

Lady Caroline. As far as I can see, he is to do nothing but pay bills and compliments.

MRS. ALLONBY. He should persistently compromise us in public, and treat us with absolute respect when we are alone. And yet he should be always ready to have a perfectly terrible scene, whenever we want one, and to become miserable, absolutely miserable, at a moment's notice, and to overwhelm us with just reproaches in less than twenty minutes, and to be positively violent at the end of half an hour, and to leave us for ever at a quarter to eight, when we have to go and dress for dinner. And when, after that, one has seen him for really the last time, and he has refused to take back the little things he has given one, and promised never to communicate with one again, or to write one any foolish letters, he should be perfectly broken-hearted, and telegraph to one all day long, and send one little notes every half-hour by a private hansom, and dine quite alone at the club, so that every one should know how unhappy he was. And after a whole dreadful week, during which one has gone about everywhere with one's husband, just to show how absolutely lonely one was, he may be given a third last parting, in the evening, and then, if his conduct has been quite irreproachable, and one has behaved really badly to him, he should be allowed to admit that he has been entirely in the wrong, and when he has admitted that, it becomes a woman's duty to forgive, and one can do it all over again from the beginning, with variations.

LADY HUNSTANTON. How clever you are, my dear! You never mean a single word you say.

LADY STUTFIELD. Thank you, thank you. It has been quite, quite entrancing. I must try and remember it all. There are such a number of details that are so very, very important.

LADY CAROLINE. But you have not told us yet what the reward of the Ideal Man is to be.

MRS. ALLONBY. His reward? Oh, infinite expectation. That is quite enough for him.

LADY STUTFIELD. But men are so terribly, terribly exacting, are they not?

MRS. ALLONBY. That makes no matter. One should never surrender.

LADY STUTFIELD. Not even to the Ideal Man?

MRS. ALLONBY. Certainly not to him. Unless, of course, one wants to grow tired of him.

LADY STUTFIELD. Oh! . . . yes. I see that. It is very, very helpful. Do you think, Mrs. Allonby, I shall ever meet the Ideal Man? Or are there more than one?

MRS. ALLONBY. There are just four in London, Lady Stutfield.

LADY HUNSTANTON. Oh, my dear!

MRS. ALLONBY. [*Going over to her.*] What has happened? Do tell me.

LADY HUNSTANTON [*in a low voice*] I had completely forgotten that the American young lady has been in the room all the time. I am afraid some of this clever talk may have shocked her a little.

MRS. ALLONBY. Ah, that will do her so much good!

LADY HUNSTANTON. Let us hope she didn't understand much. I think I had better go over and talk to her. [*Rises and goes across to*HESTER WORSLEY.] Well, dear Miss Worsley. [*Sitting down beside her.*] How quiet you have been in your nice little corner all this time! I suppose you have been reading a book? There are so many books here in the library.

HESTER. No, I have been listening to the conversation.

LADY HUNSTANTON. You mustn't believe everything that was said, you know, dear.

HESTER. I didn't believe any of it

LADY HUNSTANTON. That is quite right, dear.

HESTER. [*Continuing.*] I couldn't believe that any women could really hold such views of life as I have heard to-night from some of your guests. [*An awkward pause.*]

LADY HUNSTANTON. I hear you have such pleasant society in America. Quite like our own in places, my son wrote to me.

HESTER. There are cliques in America as elsewhere, Lady Hunstanton. But true American society consists simply of all the good women and good men we have in our country.

LADY HUNSTANTON. What a sensible system, and I dare say quite pleasant too. I am afraid in England we have too many artificial social barriers. We don't see as much as we should of the middle and lower classes.

HESTER. In America we have no lower classes.

LADY HUNSTANTON. Really? What a very strange arrangement!

MRS. ALLONBY. What is that dreadful girl talking about?

LADY STUTFIELD. She is painfully natural, is she not?

LADY CAROLINE. There are a great many things you haven't got in America, I am told, Miss Worsley. They say you have no ruins, and no curiosities.

MRS. ALLONBY. [*To* LADY STUTFIELD.] What nonsense! They have their mothers and their manners.

HESTER. The English aristocracy supply us with our curiosities, Lady Caroline. They are sent over to us every summer, regularly, in the steamers, and propose to us the day after they land. As for ruins, we are trying to build up something that will last longer than brick or stone. [*Gets up to take her fan from table.*]

LADY HUNSTANTON. What is that, dear? Ah, yes, an iron Exhibition, is it not, at that place that has the curious name?

HESTER. [*Standing by table.*] We are trying to build up life, Lady Hunstanton, on a better, truer, purer basis than life rests on here. This sounds strange to you all, no doubt. How could it sound other than strange? You rich people in England, you don't know how you are living. How could you know? You shut out from your society the gentle and the good. You laugh at the simple and the pure. Living, as you all do, on others and by them, you sneer at self-sacrifice, and if you throw bread to the poor, it is merely to keep them quiet for a season. With all your pomp and wealth and art you don't know how to live—you don't even know that. You love the beauty that you can see and touch and handle, the beauty that you can destroy, and do destroy, but of the unseen beauty of life, of the unseen beauty of a higher life, you know nothing. You have lost life's secret. Oh, your English society seems to me shallow, selfish, foolish. It has blinded its eyes, and stopped its ears. It lies like a leper in purple. It sits like a dead thing smeared with gold. It is all wrong, all wrong.

LADY STUTFIELD. I don't think one should know of these things. It is not very, very nice, is it?

LADY HUNSTANTON. My dear Miss Worsley, I thought you liked English society so much. You were such a success in it. And you were so much admired by the best people. I quite forget what Lord Henry Weston said of you—but it was most complimentary, and you know what an authority he is on beauty.

HESTER. Lord Henry Weston! I remember him, Lady Hunstanton. A man with a hideous smile and a hideous past. He is asked everywhere. No dinner-party is complete without him. What of those whose ruin is due to him? They are outcasts. They are nameless. If you met them in the street you would turn your head away. I don't complain of their punishment. Let all women who have sinned be punished.

[MRS. ARBUTHNOT *enters from terrace behind in a cloak with a lace veil over her head. She hears the last words and starts.*]

LADY HUNSTANTON. My dear young lady!

HESTER. It is right that they should be punished, but don't let them be the only ones to suffer. If a man and woman have sinned, let them both go forth into the desert to love or loathe each other there. Let them both be branded. Set a mark, if you wish, on each, but don't punish the one and let the other go free. Don't have one law for men and another for women. You are unjust to women in England. And till you count what is a shame in a woman to be an infamy in a man, you will always be unjust, and Right, that pillar of fire, and Wrong, that pillar of cloud, will be made dim to your eyes, or be not seen at all, or if seen, not regarded.

LADY CAROLINE. Might I, dear Miss Worsley, as you are standing up, ask you for my cotton that is just behind you? Thank you.

LADY HUNSTANTON. My dear Mrs. Arbuthnot! I am so pleased you have come up. But I didn't hear you announced.

MRS. ALLONBY. Oh, I came straight in from the terrace, Lady Hunstanton, just as I was. You didn't tell me you had a party.

LADY HUNSTANTON. Not a party. Only a few guests who are staying in the house, and whom you must know. Allow me. [*Tries to help her. Rings bell.*] Caroline, this is Mrs. Arbuthnot, one of my sweetest friends. Lady Caroline Pontefract, Lady Stutfield, Mrs. Allonby, and my young American friend, Miss Worsley, who has just been telling us all how wicked we are.

HESTER. I am afraid you think I spoke too strongly, Lady Hunstanton. But there are some things in England—

LADY HUNSTANTON. My dear young lady, there was a great deal of truth, I dare say, in what you said, and you looked very pretty while you said it, which is much more important, Lord Illingworth would tell us. The only point where I thought you were a little hard was about Lady Caroline's brother, about poor Lord Henry. He is really such good company.

[*Enter Footman.*]

Take Mrs. Arbuthnot's things.

[*Exit Footman with wraps.*]

HESTER. Lady Caroline, I had no idea it was your brother. I am sorry for the pain I must have caused you—I—

LADY CAROLINE. My dear Miss Worsley, the only part of your little speech, if I may so term it, with which I thoroughly agreed, was the part about my brother. Nothing that you could possibly say could be too bad for him. I regard Henry as infamous, absolutely infamous. But I am bound to state, as you were remarking, Jane, that he is excellent company, and he has one of the best cooks in London, and after a good dinner one can forgive anybody, even one's own relations.

LADY HUNSTANTON [*to* MISS WORSLEY] Now, do come, dear, and make friends with Mrs. Arbuthnot. She is one of the good, sweet, simple people you told us we never admitted into society. I am sorry to say Mrs. Arbuthnot comes very rarely to me. But that is not my fault.

MRS. ALLONBY. What a bore it is the men staying so long after dinner! I expect they are saying the most dreadful things about us.

LADY STUTFIELD. Do you really think so?

MRS. ALLONBY. I was sure of it.

LADY STUTFIELD. How very, very horrid of them! Shall we go onto the terrace?

MRS. ALLONBY. Oh, anything to get away from the dowagers and the dowdies. [*Rises and goes with* LADY STUTFIELD *to door* L.C.] We are only going to look at the stars, Lady Hunstanton.

LADY HUNSTANTON. You will find a great many, dear, a great many. But don't catch cold. [*To* MRS. ARBUTHNOT.] We shall all miss Gerald so much, dear Mrs. Arbuthnot.

MRS. ARBUTHNOT. But has Lord Illingworth really offered to make Gerald his secretary?

LADY HUNSTANTON. Oh, yes! He has been most charming about it. He has the highest possible opinion of your boy. You don't know Lord Illingworth, I believe, dear.

MRS. ARBUTHNOT. I have never met him.

LADY HUNSTANTON. You know him by name, no doubt?

MRS. ARBUTHNOT. I am afraid I don't. I live so much out of the world, and see so few people. I remember hearing years ago of an old Lord Illingworth who lived in Yorkshire, I think.

LADY HUNSTANTON. Ah, yes. That would be the last Earl but one. He was a very curious man. He wanted to marry beneath him. Or wouldn't, I believe. There was some scandal about it. The present Lord Illingworth is quite different. He is very distinguished. He does—well, he does nothing, which I am afraid our pretty American visitor here thinks very wrong of anybody, and I don't know that he cares much for the subjects in which you are so interested, dear Mrs. Arbuthnot. Do you think, Caroline, that Lord Illingworth is interested in the Housing of the Poor?

LADY CAROLINE. I should fancy not at all, Jane.

LADY HUNSTANTON. We all have our different tastes, have we not? But Lord Illingworth has a very high position, and there is nothing he couldn't get if he chose to ask for it. Of course, he is comparatively a young man still, and he has only come to his title within—how long exactly is it, Caroline, since Lord Illingworth succeeded?

LADY CAROLINE. About four years, I think, Jane. I know it was the same year in which my brother had his last exposure in the evening newspapers.

LADY HUNSTANTON. Ah, I remember. That would be about four years ago. Of course, there were a great many people between the present Lord Illingworth and the title, Mrs. Arbuthnot. There was—who was there, Caroline?

LADY CAROLINE. There was poor Margaret's baby. You remember how anxious she was to have a boy, and it was a boy, but it died, and her husband died shortly afterwards, and she married almost immediately one of Lord Ascot's sons, who, I am told, beats her.

LADY HUNSTANTON. Ah, that is in the family, dear, that is in the family. And there was also, I remember, a clergyman who wanted to be a lunatic, or a lunatic who wanted to be a clergyman, I forget which, but I know the Court of Chancery investigated the matter, and decided that he was quite sane. And I saw him afterwards at poor Lord Plumstead's with straws in his hair, or something very odd about him. I can't recall what. I often regret, Lady Caroline, that dear Lady Cecilia never lived to see her son get the title.

MRS. ARBUTHNOT. Lady Cecilia?

LADY HUNSTANTON. Lord Illingworth's mother, dear Mrs. Arbuthnot, was one of the Duchess of Jerningham's pretty daughters, and she married Sir Thomas Harford, who wasn't considered a very good match for her at the time, though he was said to be the handsomest man in London. I knew them all quite intimately, and both the sons, Arthur and George.

MRS. ARBUTHNOT. It was the eldest son who succeeded, of course, Lady Hunstanton?

LADY HUNSTANTON. No, dear, he was killed in the hunting field. Or was it fishing, Caroline? I forget. But George came in for everything. I always tell him that no younger son has ever had such good luck as he has had.

MRS. ARBUTHNOT. Lady Hunstanton, I want to speak to Gerald at once. Might I see him? Can he be sent for?

LADY HUNSTANTON. Certainly, dear. I will send one of the servants into the dining-room to fetch him. I don't know what keeps the gentlemen so long. [*Rings bell.*] When I knew Lord Illingworth first as plain George Harford, he was simply a very brilliant young man about town, with not a penny of money except what poor dear Lady Cecilia gave him. She was quite devoted to him. Chiefly, I fancy, because he was on bad terms with his father. Oh, here is the dear Archdeacon. [*To Servant.*] It doesn't matter.

[*Enter* SIR JOHN *and* DOCTOR DAUBENY. SIR JOHN *goes over to* LADY STUTFIELD, DOCTOR DAUBENY *to* LADY HUNSTANTON.]

THE ARCHDEACON. Lord Illingworth has been most entertaining. I have never enjoyed myself more. [*Sees* MRS. ARBUTHNOT.] Ah, Mrs. Arbuthnot.

LADY HUNSTANTON. [*To* DOCTOR BAUBENY.] You see I have got Mrs. Arbuthnot to come to me at last.

THE ARCHDEACON. That is a great honour, Lady Hunstanton. Mrs. Daubeny will be quite jealous of you.

LADY HUNSTANTON. Ah, I am so sorry Mrs. Daubeny could not come with you to-night. Headache as usual, I suppose.

THE ARCHDEACON. Yes, Lady Hunstanton; a perfect martyr. But she is happiest alone. She is happiest alone.

LADY CAROLINE. [*To her husband.*] John! [SIR JOHN *goes over to his wife.* DOCTOR BAUBENY *talks to* LADY HUNSTANTON *and* MRS. ARBUTHNOT.]

[MRS. ARBUTHNOT watches LORD ILLINGWORTH the whole time. He has passed across the room without noticing her, and approaches MRS. ALLONBY, who with LADY STUTFIELD is standing by the door looking on to the terrace.]

LORD ILLINGWORTH. How is the most charming woman in the world?

MRS. ALLONBY. [Taking LADY STUTFIELD by the hand.] We are both quite well, thank you, Lord Illingworth. But what a short time you have been in the dining-room! It seems as if we had only just left.

LORD ILLINGWORTH. I was bored to death. Never opened my lips the whole time. Absolutely longing to come in to you.

MRS. ALLONBY. You should have. The American girl has been giving us a lecture.

LORD ILLINGWORTH. Really? All Americans lecture, I believe. I suppose it is something in their climate. What did she lecture about?

MRS. ALLONBY. Oh, Puritanism, of course.

LORD ILLINGWORTH. I am going to convert her, am I not? How long do you give me?

MRS. ALLONBY. A week.

LORD ILLINGWORTH. A week is more than enough.

[*Enter* GERALD *and* LORD ALFRED.]

GERALD. [*Going to* MRS. ARBUTHNOT.] Dear mother!

MRS. ARBUTHNOT. Gerald, I don't feel at all well. See me home, Gerald. I shouldn't have come.

GERALD. I am so sorry, mother. Certainly. But you must know Lord Illingworth first. [*Goes across room.*]

MRS. ARBUTHNOT. Not to-night, Gerald.

GERALD. Lord Illingworth, I want you so much to know my mother.

LORD ILLINGWORTH. With the greatest pleasure. [*To* MRS. ALLONBY.] I'll be back in a moment. People's mothers always bore me to death. All women become like their mothers. That is their tragedy.

MRS. ALLONBY. No man does. That is his.

LORD ILLINGWORTH. What a delightful mood you are in to-night! [*Turns round and goes across with* GERALD *to* MRS. ARBUTHNOT. *When he sees her, he starts back in wonder. Then slowly his eyes turn towards* GERALD.]

GERALD. Mother, this is Lord Illingworth, who has offered to take me as his private secretary. [MRS. ARBUTHNOT *bows coldly*.] It is a wonderful opening for me, isn't it? I hope he won't be disappointed in me, that is all. You'll thank Lord Illingworth, mother, won't you?

MRS. ARBUTHNOT. Lord Illingworth in very good, I am sure, to interest himself in you for the moment.

LORD ILLINGWORTH. [*Putting his hand on* GERALD'S *shoulder*.] Oh, Gerald and I are great friends already, Mrs . . . Arbuthnot.

MRS. ARBUTHNOT. There can be nothing in common between you and my son, Lord Illingworth.

GERALD. Dear mother, how can you say so? Of course Lord Illingworth is awfully clever and that sort of thing. There is nothing Lord Illingworth doesn't know.

LORD ILLINGWORTH. My dear boy!

GERALD. He knows more about life than any one I have ever met. I feel an awful duffer when I am with you, Lord Illingworth. Of course, I have had so few advantages. I have not been to Eton or Oxford like other chaps. But Lord Illingworth doesn't seem to mind that. He has been awfully good to me, mother.

MRS. ARBUTHNOT. Lord Illingworth may change his mind. He may not really want you as his secretary.

GERALD. Mother!

MRS. ARBUTHNOT. You must remember, as you said yourself, you have had so few advantages.

MRS. ALLONBY. Lord Illingworth, I want to speak to you for a moment. Do come over.

LORD ILLINGWORTH. Will you excuse me, Mrs. Arbuthnot? Now, don't let your charming mother make any more difficulties, Gerald. The thing is quite settled, isn't it?

GERALD. I hope so. [LORD ILLINGWORTH *goes across to* MRS. ARBUTHNOT.]

MRS. ALLONBY. I thought you were never going to leave the lady in black velvet.

LORD ILLINGWORTH. She is excessively handsome. [*Looks at* MRS. ARBUTHNOT.]

LADY HUNSTANTON. Caroline, shall we all make a move to the music-room? Miss Worsley is going to play. You'll come too, dear Mrs. Arbuthnot, won't you? You don't know what a treat is in store for you. [*To* DOCTOR BAUBENY.] I must really take Miss Worsley down some afternoon to the rectory. I should so much like dear Mrs. Daubeny to hear her on the violin. Ah, I forgot. Dear Mrs. Daubeny's hearing is a little defective, is it not?

THE ARCHDEACON. Her deafness is a great privation to her. She can't even hear my sermons now. She reads them at home. But she has many resources in herself, many resources.

LADY HUNSTANTON. She reads a good deal, I suppose?

THE ARCHDEACON. Just the very largest print. The eyesight is rapidly going. But she's never morbid, never morbid.

GERALD. [*To* LORD ILLINGWORTH.] Do speak to my mother, Lord Illingworth, before you go into the music-room. She seems to think, somehow, you don't mean what you said to me.

MRS. ALLONBY. Aren't you coming?

LORD ILLINGWORTH. In a few moments. Lady Hunstanton, if Mrs. Arbuthnot would allow me, I would like to say a few words to her, and we will join you later on.

LADY HUNSTANTON. Ah, of course. You will have a great deal to say to her, and she will have a great deal to thank you for. It is not every son who gets such an offer, Mrs. Arbuthnot. But I know you appreciate that, dear.

LADY CAROLINE. John!

LADY HUNSTANTON. Now, don't keep Mrs. Arbuthnot too long, Lord Illingworth. We can't spare her.

[*Exit following the other guests. Sound of violin heard from music-room.*]

LORD ILLINGWORTH. So that is our son, Rachel! Well, I am very proud of him. He in a Harford, every inch of him. By the way, why Arbuthnot, Rachel?

MRS. ARBUTHNOT. One name is as good as another, when one has no right to any name.

LORD ILLINGWORTH. I suppose so—but why Gerald?

MRS. ARBUTHNOT. After a man whose heart I broke—after my father.

LORD ILLINGWORTH. Well, Rachel, what in over is over. All I have got to say now in that I am very, very much pleased with our boy. The world will know him merely as my private secretary, but to me he will be something very near, and very dear. It is a curious thing, Rachel; my life seemed to be quite complete. It was not so. It lacked something, it lacked a son. I have found my son now, I am glad I have found him.

MRS. ARBUTHNOT. You have no right to claim him, or the smallest part of him. The boy is entirely mine, and shall remain mine.

LORD ILLINGWORTH. My dear Rachel, you have had him to yourself for over twenty years. Why not let me have him for a little now? He is quite as much mine as yours.

MRS. ARBUTHNOT. Are you talking of the child you abandoned? Of the child who, as far as you are concerned, might have died of hunger and of want?

LORD ILLINGWORTH. You forget, Rachel, it was you who left me. It was not I who left you.

MRS. ARBUTHNOT. I left you because you refused to give the child a name. Before my son was born, I implored you to marry me.

LORD ILLINGWORTH. I had no expectations then. And besides, Rachel, I wasn't much older than you were. I was only twenty-two. I was twenty-one, I believe, when the whole thing began in your father's garden.

MRS. ARBUTHNOT. When a man is old enough to do wrong he should be old enough to do right also.

LORD ILLINGWORTH. My dear Rachel, intellectual generalities are always interesting, but generalities in morals mean absolutely nothing. As for saying I left our child to starve, that, of course, is untrue and silly. My mother offered you six hundred a year. But you wouldn't take anything. You simply disappeared, and carried the child away with you.

MRS. ARBUTHNOT. I wouldn't have accepted a penny from her. Your father was different. He told you, in my presence, when we were in Paris, that it was your duty to marry me.

LORD ILLINGWORTH. Oh, duty is what one expects from others, it is not what one does oneself. Of course, I was influenced by my mother. Every man is when he is young.

MRS. ARBUTHNOT. I am glad to hear you say so. Gerald shall certainly not go away with you.

LORD ILLINGWORTH. What nonsense, Rachel!

MRS. ARBUTHNOT. Do you think I would allow my son—

LORD ILLINGWORTH. *Our* son.

MRS. ARBUTHNOT. My son [LORD ILLINGWORTH *shrugs his shoulders*]—to go away with the man who spoiled my youth, who ruined my life, who has tainted every moment of my days? You don't realise what my past has been in suffering and in shame.

LORD ILLINGWORTH. My dear Rachel, I must candidly say that I think Gerald's future considerably more important than your past.

MRS. ARBUTHNOT. Gerald cannot separate his future from my past.

LORD ILLINGWORTH. That is exactly what he should do. That is exactly what you should help him to do. What a typical woman you are! You talk sentimentally, and you are thoroughly selfish the whole time. But don't let us have a scene. Rachel, I want you to look at this matter from the common-sense point of view, from the point of view of what is best for our son, leaving you and me out of the question. What is our son at present? An underpaid clerk in a small Provincial Bank in a third-rate English town. If you imagine he is quite happy in such a position, you are mistaken. He is thoroughly discontented.

MRS. ARBUTHNOT. He was not discontented till he met you. You have made him so.

LORD ILLINGWORTH. Of course, I made him so. Discontent is the first step in the progress of a man or a nation. But I did not leave him with a mere longing for things he could not get. No, I made him a charming offer. He jumped at it, I need hardly say. Any young man would. And now, simply because it turns out that I am the boy's own father and he my own son, you propose practically to ruin his career. That is to say, if I were a perfect stranger, you would allow Gerald to go away with me, but as he is my own flesh and blood you won't. How utterly illogical you are!

MRS. ARBUTHNOT. I will not allow him to go.

LORD ILLINGWORTH. How can you prevent it? What excuse can you give to him for making him decline such an offer as mine? I won't tell him in what relations I stand to him, I need hardly say. But you daren't tell him. You know that. Look how you have brought him up.

MRS. ARBUTHNOT. I have brought him up to be a good man.

LORD ILLINGWORTH. Quite so. And what is the result? You have educated him to be your judge if he ever finds you out. And a bitter, an unjust judge he will be to you. Don't be deceived, Rachel. Children begin by loving their parents. After a time they judge them. Rarely, if ever, do they forgive them.

MRS. ARBUTHNOT. George, don't take my son away from me. I have had twenty years of sorrow, and I have only had one thing to love me, only one thing to love. You have had a life of joy, and pleasure, and success. You have been quite happy, you have never thought of us. There was no reason, according to your views of life, why you should have remembered us at all. Your meeting us was a mere accident, a horrible accident. Forget it. Don't come now, and rob me of . . . of all I have in the whole world. You are so rich in other things. Leave me the little vineyard of my life; leave me the walled-in garden and the well of water; the ewe-lamb God sent me, in pity or in wrath, oh! leave me that. George, don't take Gerald from me.

LORD ILLINGWORTH. Rachel, at the present moment you are not necessary to Gerald's career; I am. There is nothing more to be said on the subject.

MRS. ARBUTHNOT. I will not let him go.

LORD ILLINGWORTH. Here is Gerald. He has a right to decide for himself.

[*Enter* GERALD.]

GERALD. Well, dear mother, I hope you have settled it all with Lord Illingworth?

MRS. ARBUTHNOT. I have not, Gerald.

LORD ILLINGWORTH. Your mother seems not to like your coming with me, for some reason.

GERALD. Why, mother?

MRS. ARBUTHNOT. I thought you were quite happy here with me, Gerald. I didn't know you were so anxious to leave me.

GERALD. Mother, how can you talk like that? Of course I have been quite happy with you. But a man can't stay always with his mother. No chap does. I want to make myself a position, to do something. I thought you would have been proud to see me Lord Illingworth's secretary.

MRS. ARBUTHNOT. I do not think you would be suitable as a private secretary to Lord Illingworth. You have no qualifications.

LORD ILLINGWORTH. I don't wish to seem to interfere for a moment, Mrs. Arbuthnot, but as far as your last objection is concerned, I surely am the best judge. And I can only tell you that your son has all the qualifications I had hoped for. He has more, in fact, than I had even thought of. Far more. [MRS. ARBUTHNOT *remains silent.*] Have you any other reason, Mrs. Arbuthnot, why you don't wish your son to accept this post?

GERALD. Have you, mother? Do answer.

LORD ILLINGWORTH. If you have, Mrs. Arbuthnot, pray, pray say it. We are quite by ourselves here. Whatever it is, I need not say I will not repeat it.

GERALD. Mother?

LORD ILLINGWORTH. If you would like to be alone with your son, I will leave you. You may have some other reason you don't wish me to hear.

MRS. ARBUTHNOT. I have no other reason.

LORD ILLINGWORTH. Then, my dear boy, we may look on the thing as settled. Come, you and I will smoke a cigarette on the terrace together. And Mrs. Arbuthnot, pray let me tell you, that I think you have acted very, very wisely.

[*Exit with* GERALD. MRS. ARBUTHNOT *is left alone. She stands immobile with a look of unutterable sorrow on her face.*]

ACT DROP

THIRD ACT

SCENE

The Picture Gallery at Hunstanton. Door at back leading on to terrace.

[LORD ILLINGWORTH *and* GERALD, R.C. LORD ILLINGWORTH *lolling on a sofa.* GERALD *in a chair.*]

LORD ILLINGWORTH. Thoroughly sensible woman, your mother, Gerald. I knew she would come round in the end.

GERALD. My mother is awfully conscientious, Lord Illingworth, and I know she doesn't think I am educated enough to be your secretary. She is perfectly right, too. I was fearfully idle when I was at school, and I couldn't pass an examination now to save my life.

LORD ILLINGWORTH. My dear Gerald, examinations are of no value whatsoever. If a man is a gentleman, he knows quite enough, and if he is not a gentleman, whatever he knows is bad for him.

GERALD. But I am so ignorant of the world, Lord Illingworth.

LORD ILLINGWORTH. Don't be afraid, Gerald. Remember that you've got on your side the most wonderful thing in the world—youth! There is nothing like youth. The middle-aged are mortgaged to Life. The old are in life's lumber-room. But youth is the Lord of Life. Youth has a kingdom waiting for it. Every one is born a king, and most people die in exile, like most kings. To win back my youth, Gerald, there is nothing I wouldn't do—except take exercise, get up early, or be a useful member of the community.

GERALD. But you don't call yourself old, Lord Illingworth?

LORD ILLINGWORTH. I am old enough to be your father, Gerald.

GERALD. I don't remember my father; he died years ago.

LORD ILLINGWORTH. So Lady Hunstanton told me.

GERALD. It is very curious, my mother never talks to me about my father. I sometimes think she must have married beneath her.

LORD ILLINGWORTH. [*Winces slightly.*] Really? [*Goes over and puts his hand on* GERALD'S *shoulder.*] You have missed not having a father, I suppose, Gerald?

GERALD. Oh, no; my mother has been so good to me. No one ever had such a mother as I have had.

LORD ILLINGWORTH. I am quite sure of that. Still I should imagine that most mothers don't quite understand their sons. Don't realise, I mean, that a son has ambitions, a desire to see life, to make himself a name. After all, Gerald, you couldn't be expected to pass all your life in such a hole as Wrockley, could you?

GERALD. Oh, no! It would be dreadful!

LORD ILLINGWORTH. A mother's love is very touching, of course, but it is often curiously selfish. I mean, there is a good deal of selfishness in it.

GERALD. [*Slowly.*] I suppose there is.

LORD ILLINGWORTH. Your mother is a thoroughly good woman. But good women have such limited views of life, their horizon is so small, their interests are so petty, aren't they?

GERALD. They are awfully interested, certainly, in things we don't care much about.

LORD ILLINGWORTH. I suppose your mother is very religious, and that sort of thing.

GERALD. Oh, yes, she's always going to church.

LORD ILLINGWORTH. Ah! she is not modern, and to be modern is the only thing worth being nowadays. You want to be modern, don't you, Gerald? You want to know life as it really is. Not to be put of with any old-fashioned theories about life. Well, what you have to do at present is simply to fit yourself for the best society. A man who can dominate a London dinner-table can dominate the world. The future belongs to the dandy. It is the exquisites who are going to rule.

GERALD. I should like to wear nice things awfully, but I have always been told that a man should not think too much about his clothes.

LORD ILLINGWORTH. People nowadays are so absolutely superficial that they don't understand the philosophy of the superficial. By the way, Gerald, you should learn how to tie your tie better.
Sentiment is all very well for the button-hole. But

the essential thing for a necktie is style. A well-tied tie is the first serious step in life.

GERALD. [*Laughing.*] I might be able to learn how to tie a tie, Lord Illingworth, but I should never be able to talk as you do. I don't know how to talk.

LORD ILLINGWORTH. Oh! talk to every woman as if you loved her, and to every man as if he bored you, and at the end of your first season you will have the reputation of possessing the most perfect social tact.

GERALD. But it is very difficult to get into society isn't it?

LORD ILLINGWORTH. To get into the best society, nowadays, one has either to feed people, amuse people, or shock people—that is all!

GERALD. I suppose society is wonderfully delightful!

LORD ILLINGWORTH. To be in it is merely a bore. But to be out of it simply a tragedy. Society is a necessary thing. No man has any real success in this world unless he has got women to back him, and women rule society. If you have not got women on your side you are quite over. You might just as well be a barrister, or a stockbroker, or a journalist at once.

GERALD. It is very difficult to understand women, is it not?

LORD ILLINGWORTH. You should never try to understand them. Women are pictures. Men are problems. If you want to know what a woman really means—which, by the way, is always a dangerous thing to do—look at her, don't listen to her.

GERALD. But women are awfully clever, aren't they?

LORD ILLINGWORTH. One should always tell them so. But, to the philosopher, my dear Gerald, women represent the triumph of matter over mind—just as men represent the triumph of mind over morals.

GERALD. How then can women have so much power as you say they have?

LORD ILLINGWORTH. The history of women is the history of the worst form of tyranny the world has ever known. The tyranny of the weak over the strong. It is the only tyranny that lasts.

GERALD. But haven't women got a refining influence?

LORD ILLINGWORTH. Nothing refines but the intellect.

GERALD. Still, there are many different kinds of women, aren't there?

LORD ILLINGWORTH. Only two kinds in society: the plain and the coloured.

GERALD. But there are good women in society, aren't there?

LORD ILLINGWORTH. Far too many.

GERALD. But do you think women shouldn't be good?

LORD ILLINGWORTH. One should never tell them so, they'd all become good at once. Women are a fascinatingly wilful sex. Every woman is a rebel, and usually in wild revolt against herself.

GERALD. You have never been married, Lord Illingworth, have you?

LORD ILLINGWORTH. Men marry because they are tired; women because they are curious. Both are disappointed.

GERALD. But don't you think one can be happy when one is married?

LORD ILLINGWORTH. Perfectly happy. But the happiness of a married man, my dear Gerald, depends on the people he has not married.

GERALD. But if one is in love?

LORD ILLINGWORTH. One should always be in love. That is the reason one should never marry.

GERALD. Love is a very wonderful thing, isn't it?

LORD ILLINGWORTH. When one is in love one begins by deceiving oneself. And one ends by deceiving others. That is what the world calls a romance. But a really *grande passion* is comparatively rare nowadays. It is the privilege of people who have nothing to do. That is the one use of the idle classes in a country, and the only possible explanation of us Harfords.

GERALD. Harfords, Lord Illingworth?

LORD ILLINGWORTH. That is my family name. You should study the Peerage, Gerald. It is the one book a young man about town should know thoroughly, and it is the best thing in fiction the English have ever done. And now, Gerald, you are going into a perfectly new life with me, and I want you to know how to live. [MRS. ARBUTHNOT *appears on terrace behind.*] For the world has been made by fools that wise men should live in it!

[*Enter* L.C. LADY HUNSTANTON *and* DR. DAUBENY.]

LADY HUNSTANTON. Ah! here you are, dear Lord Illingworth. Well, I suppose you have been telling our young friend, Gerald, what his new duties are to be, and giving him a great deal of good advice over a pleasant cigarette.

LORD ILLINGWORTH. I have been giving him the best of advice, Lady Hunstanton, and the best of cigarettes.

LADY HUNSTANTON. I am so sorry I was not here to listen to you, but I suppose I am too old now to learn. Except from you, dear Archdeacon, when you are in your nice pulpit. But then I always know what you are going to say, so I don't feel alarmed.

[*Sees* MRS. ARBUTHNOT.] Ah! dear Mrs. Arbuthnot, do come and join us. Come, dear. [*Enter* MRS. ARBUTHNOT.] Gerald has been having such a long talk with Lord Illingworth; I am sure you must feel very much flattered at the pleasant way in which everything has turned out for him. Let us sit down. [*They sit down.*] And how is your beautiful embroidery going on?

MRS. ARBUTHNOT. I am always at work, Lady Hunstanton.

LADY HUNSTANTON. Mrs. Daubeny embroiders a little, too, doesn't she?

THE ARCHDEACON. She was very deft with her needle once, quite a Dorcas. But the gout has crippled her fingers a good deal. She has not touched the tambour frame for nine or ten years. But she has many other amusements. She is very much interested in her own health.

LADY HUNSTANTON. Ah! that is always a nice distraction, in it not? Now, what are you talking about, Lord Illingworth? Do tell us.

LORD ILLINGWORTH. I was on the point of explaining to Gerald that the world has always laughed at its own tragedies, that being the only way in which it has been able to bear them. And that, consequently, whatever the world has treated seriously belongs to the comedy side of things.

LADY HUNSTANTON. Now I am quite out of my depth. I usually am when Lord Illingworth says anything. And the Humane Society is most careless. They never rescue me. I am left to sink. I have a dim idea, dear Lord Illingworth, that you are always on the side of the sinners, and I know I always try to be on the side of the saints, but that is as far as I get. And after all, it may be merely the fancy of a drowning person.

LORD ILLINGWORTH. The only difference between the saint and the sinner is that every saint has a past, and every sinner has a future.

LADY HUNSTANTON. Ah! that quite does for me. I haven't a word to say. You and I, dear Mrs. Arbuthnot, are behind the age. We can't follow Lord Illingworth. Too much care was taken with our education, I am afraid. To have been well brought up is a great drawback nowadays. It shuts one out from so much.

MRS. ARBUTHNOT. I should be sorry to follow Lord Illingworth in any of his opinions.

LADY HUNSTANTON. You are quite right, dear.

[GERALD *shrugs his shoulders and looks irritably over at his mother. Enter* LADY CAROLINE.]

LADY CAROLINE. Jane, have you seen John anywhere?

LADY HUNSTANTON. You needn't be anxious about him, dear. He is with Lady Stutfield; I saw them some time ago, in the Yellow Drawing-room. They seem quite happy together. You are not going, Caroline? Pray sit down.

LADY CAROLINE. I think I had better look after John.

[*Exit* LADY CAROLINE.]

LADY HUNSTANTON. It doesn't do to pay men so much attention. And Caroline has really nothing to be anxious about. Lady Stutfield is very sympathetic. She is just as sympathetic about one thing as she is about another. A beautiful nature.

[*Enter* SIR JOHN *and* MRS. ALLONBY.]

Ah! here is Sir John! And with Mrs. Allonby too! I suppose it was Mrs. Allonby I saw him with. Sir John, Caroline has been looking everywhere for you.

MRS. ALLONBY. We have been waiting for her in the Music-room, dear Lady Hunstanton.

LADY HUNSTANTON. Ah! the Music-room, of course. I thought it was the Yellow Drawing-room, my memory is getting so defective. [*To the* ARCHDEACON.] Mrs. Daubeny has a wonderful memory, hasn't she?

THE ARCHDEACON. She used to be quite remarkable for her memory, but since her last attack she recalls chiefly the events of her early childhood. But she finds great pleasure in such retrospections, great pleasure.

[*Enter* LADY STUTFIELD *and* MR. KELVIL.]

LADY HUNSTANTON. Ah! dear Lady Stutfield! and what has Mr. Kelvil been talking to you about?

LADY STUTFIELD. About Bimetallism, as well as I remember.

LADY HUNSTANTON. Bimetallism! Is that quite a nice subject? However, I know people discuss everything very freely nowadays. What did Sir John talk to you about, dear Mrs. Allonby?

MRS. ALLONBY. About Patagonia.

LADY HUNSTANTON. Really? What a remote topic! But very improving, I have no doubt.

MRS. ALLONBY. He has been most interesting on the subject of Patagonia. Savages seem to have quite the same views as cultured people on almost all subjects. They are excessively advanced.

LADY HUNSTANTON. What do they do?

MRS. ALLONBY. Apparently everything.

LADY HUNSTANTON. Well, it is very gratifying, dear Archdeacon, is it not, to find that Human Nature is permanently one.—On the whole, the world is the same world, is it not?

LORD ILLINGWORTH. The world is simply divided into two classes—those who believe the incredible, like the public—and those who do the improbable—

MRS. ALLONBY. Like yourself?

LORD ILLINGWORTH. Yes; I am always astonishing myself. It is the only thing that makes life worth living.

LADY STUTFIELD. And what have you been doing lately that astonishes you?

LORD ILLINGWORTH. I have been discovering all kinds of beautiful qualities in my own nature.

MRS. ALLONBY. Ah! don't become quite perfect all at once. Do it gradually!

LORD ILLINGWORTH. I don't intend to grow perfect at all. At least, I hope I shan't. It would be most inconvenient. Women love us for our defects. If we have enough of them, they will forgive us everything, even our gigantic intellects.

MRS. ALLONBY. It is premature to ask us to forgive analysis. We forgive adoration; that is quite as much as should be expected from us.

[*Enter* LORD ALFRED. *He joins* LADY STUTFIELD.]

LADY HUNSTANTON. Ah! we women should forgive everything, shouldn't we, dear Mrs. Arbuthnot? I am sure you agree with me in that.

MRS. ARBUTHNOT. I do not, Lady Hunstanton. I think there are many things women should never forgive.

LADY HUNSTANTON. What sort of things?

MRS. ARBUTHNOT. The ruin of another woman's life.

[*Moves slowly away to back of stage.*]

LADY HUNSTANTON. Ah! those things are very sad, no doubt, but I believe there are admirable homes where people of that kind are looked after and reformed, and I think on the whole that the secret of life is to take things very, very easily.

MRS. ALLONBY. The secret of life is never to have an emotion that is unbecoming.

LADY STUTFIELD. The secret of life is to appreciate the pleasure of being terribly, terribly deceived.

KELVIL. The secret of life is to resist temptation, Lady Stutfield.

LORD ILLINGWORTH. There is no secret of life. Life's aim, if it has one, is simply to be always looking for temptations. There are not nearly enough. I sometimes pass a whole day without coming across a single one. It is quite dreadful. It makes one so nervous about the future.

LADY HUNSTANTON. [*Shakes her fan at him.*] I don't know how it is, dear Lord Illingworth, but everything you have said to-day seems to me excessively immoral. It has been most interesting, listening to you.

LORD ILLINGWORTH. All thought is immoral. Its very essence is destruction. If you think of anything, you kill it. Nothing survives being thought of.

LADY HUNSTANTON. I don't understand a word, Lord Illingworth. But I have no doubt it is all quite true. Personally, I have very little to reproach myself with, on the score of thinking. I don't believe in women thinking too much. Women should think in moderation, as they should do all things in moderation.

LORD ILLINGWORTH. Moderation is a fatal thing, Lady Hunstanton. Nothing succeeds like excess.

LADY HUNSTANTON. I hope I shall remember that. It sounds an admirable maxim. But I'm beginning to forget everything. It's a great misfortune.

LORD ILLINGWORTH. It is one of your most fascinating qualities, Lady Hunstanton. No woman should have a memory. Memory in a woman is the beginning of dowdiness. One can always tell from a woman's bonnet whether she has got a memory or not.

LADY HUNSTANTON. How charming you are, dear Lord Illingworth. You always find out that one's most glaring fault is one's most important virtue. You have the most comforting views of life.

[*Enter* FARQUHAR.]

FARQUHAR. Doctor Daubeny's carriage!

LADY HUNSTANTON. My dear Archdeacon! It is only half-past ten.

THE ARCHDEACON. [*Rising.*] I am afraid I must go, Lady Hunstanton. Tuesday is always one of Mrs. Daubeny's bad nights.

LADY HUNSTANTON. [*Rising.*] Well, I won't keep you from her. [*Goes with him towards door.*] I have told Farquhar to put a brace of partridge into the carriage. Mrs. Daubeny may fancy them.

THE ARCHDEACON. It is very kind of you, but Mrs. Daubeny never touches solids now. Lives entirely on jellies. But she is wonderfully cheerful, wonderfully cheerful. She has nothing to complain of.

[*Exit with* LADY HUNSTANTON.]

MRS. ALLONBY. [*Goes over to* LORD ILLINGWORTH.] There is a beautiful moon to-night.

LORD ILLINGWORTH. Let us go and look at it. To look at anything that is inconstant is charming nowadays.

MRS. ALLONBY. You have your looking-glass.

LORD ILLINGWORTH. It is unkind. It merely shows me my wrinkles.

MRS. ALLONBY. Mine is better behaved. It never tells me the truth.

LORD ILLINGWORTH. Then it is in love with you.

[*Exeunt* SIR JOHN, LADY STUTFIELD, MR. KELVIL *and* LORD ALFRED.]

GERALD. [*To* LORD ILLINGWORTH] May I come too?

LORD ILLINGWORTH. Do, my dear boy. [*Moves towards with* MRS. ALLONBY *and* GERALD.]

[LADY CAROLINE *enters, looks rapidly round and goes off in opposite direction to that taken by* SIR JOHN *and* LADY STUTFIELD.]

MRS. ARBUTHNOT. Gerald!

GERALD. What, mother!

[*Exit* LORD ILLINGWORTH *with* MRS. ALLONBY.]

MRS. ARBUTHNOT. It is getting late. Let us go home.

GERALD. My dear mother. Do let us wait a little longer. Lord Illingworth is so delightful, and, by the way, mother, I have a great surprise for you. We are starting for India at the end of this month.

MRS. ARBUTHNOT. Let us go home.

GERALD. If you really want to, of course, mother, but I must bid good-bye to Lord Illingworth first. I'll be back in five minutes. [*Exit.*]

MRS. ARBUTHNOT. Let him leave me if he chooses, but not with him—not with him! I couldn't bear it. [*Walks up and down.*]

[*Enter* HESTER.]

HESTER. What a lovely night it is, Mrs. Arbuthnot.

MRS. ARBUTHNOT. Is it?

HESTER. Mrs. Arbuthnot, I wish you would let us be friends. You are so different from the other women here. When you came into the Drawing-room this evening, somehow you brought with you a sense of what is good and pure in life. I had been foolish. There are things that are right to say, but that may be said at the wrong time and to the wrong people.

MRS. ARBUTHNOT. I heard what you said. I agree with it, Miss Worsley.

HESTER. I didn't know you had heard it. But I knew you would agree with me. A woman who has sinned should be punished, shouldn't she?

MRS. ARBUTHNOT. Yes.

HESTER. She shouldn't be allowed to come into the society of good men and women?

MRS. ARBUTHNOT. She should not.

HESTER. And the man should be punished in the same way?

MRS. ARBUTHNOT. In the same way. And the children, if there are children, in the same way also?

HESTER. Yes, it is right that the sins of the parents should be visited on the children. It is a just law. It is God's law.

MRS. ARBUTHNOT. It is one of God's terrible laws.

[*Moves away to fireplace.*]

HESTER. You are distressed about your son leaving you, Mrs. Arbuthnot?

MRS. ARBUTHNOT. Yes.

HESTER. Do you like him going away with Lord Illingworth? Of course there is position, no doubt, and money, but position and money are not everything, are they?

MRS. ARBUTHNOT. They are nothing; they bring misery.

HESTER. Then why do you let your son go with him?

MRS. ARBUTHNOT. He wishes it himself.

HESTER. But if you asked him he would stay, would he not?

MRS. ARBUTHNOT. He has set his heart on going.

HESTER. He couldn't refuse you anything. He loves you too much. Ask him to stay. Let me send him in to you. He is on the terrace at this moment with Lord Illingworth. I heard them laughing together as I passed through the Music-room.

MRS. ARBUTHNOT. Don't trouble, Miss Worsley, I can wait. It is of no consequence.

HESTER. No, I'll tell him you want him. Do—do ask him to stay. [*Exit* HESTER.]

MRS. ARBUTHNOT. He won't come—I know he won't come.

[Enter LADY CAROLINE. *She looks round anxiously. Enter* GERALD.]

LADY CAROLINE. Mr. Arbuthnot, may I ask you is Sir John anywhere on the terrace?

GERALD. No, Lady Caroline, he is not on the terrace.

LADY CAROLINE. It is very curious. It is time for him to retire.

[*Exit* LADY CAROLINE.]

GERALD. Dear mother, I am afraid I kept you waiting. I forgot all about it. I am so happy to-night, mother; I have never been so happy.

MRS. ARBUTHNOT. At the prospect of going away?

GERALD. Don't put it like that, mother. Of course I am sorry to leave you. Why, you are the best mother in the whole world. But after all, as Lord Illingworth says, it is impossible to live in such a place as Wrockley. You don't mind it. But I'm ambitions; I want something more than that. I want to have a career. I want to do something that will make you proud of me, and Lord Illingworth is going to help me. He is going to do everything for me.

MRS. ARBUTHNOT. Gerald, don't go away with Lord Illingworth. I implore you not to. Gerald, I beg you!

GERALD. Mother, how changeable you are! You don't seem to know your own mind for a single moment. An hour and a half ago in the Drawing-room you agreed to the whole thing; now you turn round and make objections, and try to force me to give up my one chance in life. Yes, my one chance. You don't suppose that men like Lord Illingworth are to be found every day, do you, mother? It is very strange that when I have had such a wonderful piece of good luck, the one person to put difficulties in my way should be my own mother. Besides, you know, mother, I love Hester Worsley. Who could help loving her? I love her more than I have ever told you, far more. And if I had a position, if I had prospects, I could—I could ask her to—Don't you understand now, mother, what it means to me to be Lord Illingworth's secretary? To start like that is to find a career ready for one—before one—waiting for one. If I were Lord Illingworth's secretary I could ask Hester to be my wife. As a wretched bank clerk with a hundred a year it would be an impertinence.

MRS. ARBUTHNOT. I fear you need have no hopes of Miss Worsley. I know her views on life. She has just told them to me. [*A pause.*]

GERALD. Then I have my ambition left, at any rate. That is something—I am glad I have that! You have always tried to crush my ambition, mother—haven't you? You have told me that the world is a wicked place, that success is not worth having, that society is shallow, and all that sort of thing—well, I don't believe it, mother. I think the world must be delightful. I think society must be exquisite. I think success is a thing worth having. You have been wrong in all that you taught me, mother, quite wrong. Lord Illingworth is a successful man. He is a fashionable man. He is a man who lives in the world and for it. Well, I would give anything to be just like Lord Illingworth.

MRS. ARBUTHNOT. I would sooner see you dead.

GERALD. Mother, what is your objection to Lord Illingworth? Tell me—tell me right out. What is it?

MRS. ARBUTHNOT. He is a bad man.

GERALD. In what way bad? I don't understand what you mean.

MRS. ARBUTHNOT. I will tell you.

GERALD. I suppose you think him bad, because he doesn't believe the same things as you do. Well, men are different from women, mother. It is natural that they should have different views.

MRS. ARBUTHNOT. It is not what Lord Illingworth believes, or what he does not believe, that makes him bad. It is what he is.

GERALD. Mother, is it something you know of him? Something you actually know?

MRS. ARBUTHNOT. It is something I know.

GERALD. Something you are quite sure of?

MRS. ARBUTHNOT. Quite sure of.

GERALD. How long have you known it?

MRS. ARBUTHNOT. For twenty years.

GERALD. Is it fair to go back twenty years in any man's career? And what have you or I to do with Lord Illingworth's early life? What business is it of ours?

MRS. ARBUTHNOT. What this man has been, he is now, and will be always.

GERALD. Mother, tell me what Lord Illingworth did? If he did anything shameful, I will not go away with him. Surely you know me well enough for that?

MRS. ARBUTHNOT. Gerald, come near to me. Quite close to me, as you used to do when you were a little boy, when you were mother's own boy.
[GERALD *sits down betide his mother. She runs her fingers through his hair, and strokes his hands.*]
Gerald, there was a girl once, she was very young, she was little over eighteen at the time. George Harford—that was Lord Illingworth's name then—George Harford met her. She knew nothing about life. He—knew everything. He made this girl love him. He made her love him so much that she left her father's house with him one morning. She loved him

so much, and he had promised to marry her! He had solemnly promised to marry her, and she had believed him. She was very young, and—and ignorant of what life really is. But he put the marriage off from week to week, and month to month.—She trusted in him all the while. She loved him.—Before her child was born—for she had a child—she implored him for the child's sake to marry her, that the child might have a name, that her sin might not be visited on the child, who was innocent. He refused. After the child was born she left him, taking the child away, and her life was ruined, and her soul ruined, and all that was sweet, and good, and pure in her ruined also. She suffered terribly—she suffers now. She will always suffer. For her there is no joy, no peace, no atonement. She is a woman who drags a chain like a guilty thing. She is a woman who wears a mask, like a thing that is a leper. The fire cannot purify her. The waters cannot quench her anguish. Nothing can heal her! no anodyne can give her sleep! no poppies forgetfulness! She is lost! She is a lost soul!—That is why I call Lord Illingworth a bad man. That is why I don't want my boy to be with him.

GERALD. My dear mother, it all sounds very tragic, of course. But I dare say the girl was just as much to blame as Lord Illingworth was.—After all, would a really nice girl, a girl with any nice feelings at all, go away from her home with a man to whom she was not married, and live with him as his wife? No nice girl would.

MRS. ARBUTHNOT. [*After a pause.*] Gerald, I withdraw all my objections. You are at liberty to go away with Lord Illingworth, when and where you choose.

GERALD. Dear mother, I knew you wouldn't stand in my way. You are the best woman God ever made. And, as for Lord Illingworth, I don't believe he is capable of anything infamous or base. I can't believe it of him—I can't.

HESTER. [*Outside.*] Let me go! Let me go! [*Enter* HESTER *in terror, and rushes over to* GERALD *and flings herself in his arms.*]

HESTER. Oh! save me—save me from him!

GERALD. From whom?

HESTER. He has insulted me! Horribly insulted me! Save me!

GERALD. Who? Who has dared—?

[LORD ILLINGWORTH *enters at back of stage.* HESTER *breaks from* GERALD'S *arms and points to him.*]

GERALD [*He is quite beside himself with rage and indignation.*] Lord Illingworth, you have insulted the purest thing on God's earth, a thing as pure as my own mother. You have insulted the woman I love most in the world with my own mother. As there is a God in Heaven, I will kill you!

MRS. ARBUTHNOT. [*Rushing across and catching hold of him*] No! no!

GERALD. [*Thrusting her back.*] Don't hold me, mother. Don't hold me—I'll kill him!

MRS. ARBUTHNOT. Gerald!

GERALD. Let me go, I say!

MRS. ARBUTHNOT. Stop, Gerald, stop! He is your own father!

[GERALD *clutches his mother's hands and looks into her face. She sinks slowly on the ground in shame.* HESTER *steals towards the door.* LORD ILLINGWORTH *frowns and bites his lip. After a time* GERALD *raises his mother up, puts his arm round her, and leads her from the room.*]

ACT DROP

FOURTH ACT

SCENE

Sitting-room at Mrs. Arbuthnot's. Large open French window at back, looking on to garden. Doors R.C. *and* L.C.

[GERALD ARBUTHNOT *writing at table.*]

[*Enter* ALICE R.C. *followed by* LADY HUNSTANTON *and* MRS. ALLONBY.]

ALICE. Lady Hunstanton and Mrs. Allonby.

[*Exit* L.C.]

LADY HUNSTANTON. Good morning, Gerald.

GERALD. [*Rising.*] Good morning, Lady Hunstanton. Good morning, Mrs. Allonby.

LADY HUNSTANTON. [*Sitting down.*] We came to inquire for your dear mother, Gerald. I hope she is better?

GERALD. My mother has not come down yet, Lady Hunstanton.

LADY HUNSTANTON. Ah, I am afraid the heat was too much for her last night. I think there must have been thunder in the air. Or perhaps it was the music. Music makes one feel so romantic—at least it always gets on one's nerves.

MRS. ALLONBY. It's the same thing, nowadays.

LADY HUNSTANTON. I am so glad I don't know what you mean, dear. I am afraid you mean something wrong. Ah, I see you're examining Mrs. Arbuthnot's pretty room. Isn't it nice and old-fashioned?

MRS. ALLONBY. [*Surveying the room through her lorgnette.*] It looks quite the happy English home.

LADY HUNSTANTON. That's just the word, dear; that just describes it. One feels your mother's good influence in everything she has about her, Gerald.

MRS. ALLONBY. Lord Illingworth says that all influence is bad, but that a good influence is the worst in the world.

LADY HUNSTANTON. When Lord Illingworth knows Mrs. Arbuthnot better he will change his mind. I must certainly bring him here.

MRS. ALLONBY. I should like to see Lord Illingworth in a happy English home.

LADY HUNSTANTON. It would do him a great deal of good, dear. Most women in London, nowadays, seem to furnish their rooms with nothing but orchids, foreigners, and French novels. But here we have the room of a sweet saint. Fresh natural flowers, books that don't shock one, pictures that one can look at without blushing.

MRS. ALLONBY. But I like blushing.

LADY HUNSTANTON. Well, there *is* a good deal to be said for blushing, if one can do it at the proper moment. Poor dear Hunstanton used to tell me I didn't blush nearly often enough. But then he was so very particular. He wouldn't let me know any of his men friends, except those who were over seventy, like poor Lord Ashton: who afterwards, by the way, was brought into the Divorce Court. A most unfortunate case.

MRS. ALLONBY. I delight in men over seventy. They always offer one the devotion of a lifetime. I think seventy an ideal age for a man.

LADY HUNSTANTON. She is quite incorrigible, Gerald, isn't she? By-the-by, Gerald, I hope your dear mother will come and see me more often now. You and Lord Illingworth start almost immediately, don't you?

GERALD. I have given up my intention of being Lord Illingworth's secretary.

LADY HUNSTANTON. Surely not, Gerald! It would be most unwise of you. What reason can you have?

GERALD. I don't think I should be suitable for the post.

MRS. ALLONBY. I wish Lord Illingworth would ask me to be his secretary. But he says I am not serious enough.

LADY HUNSTANTON. My dear, you really mustn't talk like that in this house. Mrs. Arbuthnot doesn't know anything about the wicked society in which we all live. She won't go into it. She is far too good. I consider it was a great honour her coming to me last night. It gave quite an atmosphere of respectability to the party.

MRS. ALLONBY. Ah, that must have been what you thought was thunder in the air.

LADY HUNSTANTON. My dear, how can you say that? There is no resemblance between the two things at all. But really, Gerald, what do you mean by not being suitable?

GERALD. Lord Illingworth's views of life and mine are too different.

LADY HUNSTANTON. But, my dear Gerald, at your age you shouldn't have any views of life. They are quite out of place. You must be guided by others in this matter. Lord Illingworth has made you the most flattering offer, and travelling with him you would see the world—as much of it, at least, as one should look at—under the best auspices possible, and stay with all the right people, which is so important at this solemn moment in your career.

GERALD. I don't want to see the world: I've seen enough of it.

MRS. ALLONBY. I hope you don't think you have exhausted life, Mr. Arbuthnot. When a man says that, one knows that life has exhausted him.

GERALD. I don't wish to leave my mother.

LADY HUNSTANTON. Now, Gerald, that is pure laziness on your part. Not leave your mother! If I were your mother I would insist on your going.

[*Enter* ALICE L.C.]

ALICE. Mrs. Arbuthnot's compliments, my lady, but she has a bad headache, and cannot see any one this morning. [*Exit* R.C.]

LADY HUNSTANTON. [*Rising.*] A bad headache! I am so sorry! Perhaps you'll bring her up to Hunstanton this afternoon, if she is better, Gerald.

GERALD. I am afraid not this afternoon, Lady Hunstanton.

LADY HUNSTANTON. Well, to-morrow, then. Ah, if you had a father, Gerald, he wouldn't let you waste your life here. He would send you off with Lord Illingworth at once. But mothers are so weak. They give up to their sons in everything. We are all heart, all heart. Come, dear, I must call at the rectory and inquire for Mrs. Daubeny, who, I am afraid, is far from well. It is wonderful how the Archdeacon bears up, quite wonderful. He is the most sympathetic of husbands. Quite a model. Good-bye, Gerald, give my fondest love to your mother.

MRS. ALLONBY. Good-bye, Mr. Arbuthnot.

GERALD. Good-bye.

[*Exit* LADY HUNSTANTON *and* MRS. ALLONBY. GERALD *sits down and reads over his letter.*]

GERALD. What name can I sign? I, who have no right to any name. [*Signs name, puts letter into envelope, addresses it, and is about to seal it, when door* L.C. *opens and* MRS. ARBUTHNOT *enters.* GERALD *lays down sealing-wax. Mother and son look at each other.*]

LADY HUNSTANTON. [*Through French window at the back.*] Good-bye again, Gerald. We are taking the short cut across your pretty garden. Now, remember my advice to you—start at once with Lord Illingworth.

MRS. ALLONBY. *Au revoir*, Mr. Arbuthnot. Mind you bring me back something nice from your travels—not an Indian shawl—on no account an Indian shawl.

[*Exeunt.*]

GERALD. Mother, I have just written to him.

MRS. ARBUTHNOT. To whom?

GERALD. To my father. I have written to tell him to come here at four o'clock this afternoon.

MRS. ARBUTHNOT. He shall not come here. He shall not cross the threshold of my house.

GERALD. He must come.

MRS. ARBUTHNOT. Gerald, if you are going away with Lord Illingworth, go at once. Go before it kills me: but don't ask me to meet him.

GERALD. Mother, you don't understand. Nothing in the world would induce me to go away with Lord Illingworth, or to leave you. Surely you know me well enough for that. No: I have written to him to say—

MRS. ARBUTHNOT. What can you have to say to him?

GERALD. Can't you guess, mother, what I have written in this letter?

MRS. ARBUTHNOT. No.

GERALD. Mother, surely you can. Think, think what must be done, now, at once, within the next few days.

MRS. ARBUTHNOT. There is nothing to be done.

GERALD. I have written to Lord Illingworth to tell him that he must marry you.

MRS. ARBUTHNOT. Marry me?

GERALD. Mother, I will force him to do it. The wrong that has been done you must be repaired. Atonement must be made. Justice may be slow, mother, but it comes in the end. In a few days you shall be Lord Illingworth's lawful wife.

MRS. ARBUTHNOT. But, Gerald—

GERALD. I will insist upon his doing it. I will make him do it: he will not dare to refuse.

MRS. ARBUTHNOT. But, Gerald, it is I who refuse. I will not marry Lord Illingworth.

GERALD. Not marry him? Mother!

MRS. ARBUTHNOT. I will not marry him.

GERALD. But you don't understand: it is for your sake I am talking, not for mine. This marriage, this necessary marriage, this marriage which for obvious reasons must inevitably take place, will not help me, will not give me a name that will be really, rightly mine to bear. But surely it will be something for you, that you, my mother, should, however late, become the wife of the man who is my father. Will not that be something?

MRS. ARBUTHNOT. I will not marry him.

GERALD. Mother, you must.

MRS. ARBUTHNOT. I will not. You talk of atonement for a wrong done. What atonement can be made to me? There is no atonement possible. I am disgraced: he is not. That is all. It is the usual history of a man and a woman as it usually happens, as it always happens. And the ending is the ordinary ending. The woman suffers. The man goes free.

GERALD. I don't know if that is the ordinary ending, mother: I hope it is not. But your life, at any rate, shall not end like that. The man shall make whatever reparation is possible. It is not enough. It does not wipe out the past, I know that. But at least it makes the future better, better for you, mother.

MRS. ARBUTHNOT. I refuse to marry Lord Illingworth.

GERALD. If he came to you himself and asked you to be his wife you would give him a different answer. Remember, he is my father.

MRS. ARBUTHNOT. If he came himself, which he will not do, my answer would be the same. Remember I am your mother.

GERALD. Mother, you make it terribly difficult for me by talking like that; and I can't understand why you won't look at this matter from the right, from the only proper standpoint. It is to take away the bitterness out of your life, to take away the shadow that lies on your name, that this marriage must take place. There is no alternative: and after the marriage you and I can go away together. But the marriage must take place first. It is a duty that you owe, not merely to yourself, but to all other women—yes: to all the other women in the world, lest he betray more.

MRS. ARBUTHNOT. I owe nothing to other women. There is not one of them to help me. There is not one woman in the world to whom I could go for pity, if I would take it, or for sympathy, if I could win it. Women are hard on each other. That girl, last night, good though she is, fled from the room as though I were a tainted thing. She was right. I am a tainted thing. But my wrongs are my own, and I will bear them alone. I must bear them alone. What have women who have not sinned to do with me, or I with them? We do not understand each other.

[*Enter* HESTER *behind.*]

GERALD. I implore you to do what I ask you.

MRS. ARBUTHNOT. What son has ever asked of his mother to make so hideous a sacrifice? None.

GERALD. What mother has ever refused to marry the father of her own child? None.

MRS. ARBUTHNOT. Let me be the first, then. I will not do it.

GERALD. Mother, you believe in religion, and you brought me up to believe in it also. Well, surely your religion, the religion that you taught me when I was a boy, mother, must tell you that I am right. You know it, you feel it.

MRS. ARBUTHNOT. I do not know it. I do not feel it, nor will I ever stand before God's altar and ask God's blessing on so hideous a mockery as a marriage between me and George Harford. I will not say the words the Church bids us to say. I will not say them. I dare not. How could I swear to love the man I loathe, to honour him who wrought you dishonour, to obey him who, in his mastery, made me to sin? No: marriage is a sacrament for those who love each other. It is not for such as him, or such as me. Gerald, to save you from the world's sneers and taunts I have lied to the world. For twenty years I have lied to the world. I could not tell the world the truth. Who can, ever? But not for my own sake will I lie to God, and in God's presence. No, Gerald, no ceremony, Church-hallowed or State-made, shall ever bind me to George Harford. It may be that I am too bound to him already, who, robbing me, yet left me richer, so that in the mire of my life I found the pearl of price, or what I thought would be so.

GERALD. I don't understand you now.

MRS. ARBUTHNOT. Men don't understand what mothers are. I am no different from other women except in the wrong done me and the wrong I did, and my very heavy punishments and great disgrace. And yet, to bear you I had to look on death. To nurture you I had to wrestle with it. Death fought with me for you. All women have to fight with death to keep their children. Death, being childless, wants our children from us. Gerald, when you were naked I clothed you, when you were hungry I gave you food. Night and day all that long winter I tended you. No office is too mean, no care too lowly for the thing we women love—and oh! how *I* loved *you*. Not Hannah, Samuel more. And you needed love, for you were weakly, and only love could have kept you alive. Only love can keep any one alive. And boys are careless often and without thinking give pain, and we always fancy that when they come to man's estate and know us better they will repay us. But it is not so. The world draws them from our side, and they make friends with whom they are happier than they are with us, and have amusements from which we are barred, and interests that are not ours: and they are unjust to us often, for when they find life bitter they blame us for it, and when they find it sweet we do not taste its sweetness with them . . . You made many friends and went into their houses and were glad with them, and I, knowing my secret, did not dare to follow, but stayed at home and closed the door, shut out the sun and sat in darkness. What should I have done in honest households? My past was ever with me. . . . And you thought I didn't care for the pleasant things of life. I tell you I longed for them, but did not dare to touch them, feeling I had no right. You thought I was happier working amongst the poor. That was my mission, you imagined. It was not, but where else was I to go? The sick do not ask if the hand that smooths their pillow is pure, nor the dying care if the lips that touch their brow have known the kiss of sin. It was you I thought of all the time; I gave to them the love you did not need: lavished on them a love that was not theirs . . . And you thought I spent too much of my time in going to Church, and in Church duties. But where else could I turn? God's house is the only house where sinners are made welcome, and you were always in my heart, Gerald, too much in my heart. For, though day after day, at morn or evensong, I have knelt in God's house, I have never repented of my sin. How could I repent of my sin when you, my love, were its fruit! Even now that you are bitter to me I cannot repent. I do not. You are more to me than innocence. I would rather be your mother—oh! much rather!—than have been always pure . . . Oh, don't you see? don't you understand? It is my dishonour that has made you so dear to me. It is my disgrace that has bound you so closely to me. It is the price I paid for you—the price of soul and body—that makes me love you as I do. Oh, don't ask me to do this horrible thing. Child of my shame, be still the child of my shame!

GERALD. Mother, I didn't know you loved me so much as that. And I will be a better son to you than I have been. And you and I must never leave each other . . . but, mother . . . I can't help it . . . you must become my father's wife. You must marry him. It is your duty.

HESTER. [*Running forwards and embracing* MRS. ARBUTHNOT.] No, no; you shall not. That would be real dishonour, the first you have ever known. That would be real disgrace: the first to touch you. Leave him and come with me. There are other countries than England . . . Oh! other countries over sea, better, wiser, and less unjust lands. The world is very wide and very big.

MRS. ARBUTHNOT. No, not for me. For me the world is shrivelled to a palm's breadth, and where I walk there are thorns.

HESTER. It shall not be so. We shall somewhere find green valleys and fresh waters, and if we weep, well, we shall weep together. Have we not both loved him?

GERALD. Hester!

HESTER. [*Waving him back.*] Don't, don't! You cannot love me at all, unless you love her also. You cannot honour me, unless she's holier to you. In her all womanhood is martyred. Not she alone, but all of us are stricken in her house.

GERALD. Hester, Hester, what shall I do?

HESTER. Do you respect the man who is your father?

GERALD. Respect him? I despise him! He is infamous.

HESTER. I thank you for saving me from him last night.

GERALD. Ah, that is nothing. I would die to save you. But you don't tell me what to do now!

HESTER. Have I not thanked you for saving *me*?

GERALD. But what should I do?

HESTER. Ask your own heart, not mine. I never had a mother to save, or shame.

MRS. ARBUTHNOT. He is hard—he is hard. Let me go away.

GERALD. [*Rushes over and kneels down bedside his mother.*] Mother, forgive me: I have been to blame.

MRS. ARBUTHNOT. Don't kiss my hands: they are cold. My heart is cold: something has broken it.

HESTER. Ah, don't say that. Hearts live by being wounded. Pleasure may turn a heart to stone, riches may make it callous, but sorrow—oh, sorrow cannot break it. Besides, what sorrows have you now? Why, at this moment you are more dear to him than ever, *dear* though you have *been*, and oh! how dear you *have* been always. Ah! be kind to him.

GERALD. You are my mother and my father all in one. I need no second parent. It was for you I spoke, for you alone. Oh, say something, mother.

Have I but found one love to lose another? Don't tell me that. O mother, you are cruel. [*Gets up and flings himself sobbing on a sofa.*]

MRS. ARBUTHNOT. [*To* HESTER.] But has he found indeed another love?

HESTER. You know I have loved him always.

MRS. ARBUTHNOT. But we are very poor.

HESTER. Who, being loved, is poor? Oh, no one. I hate my riches. They are a burden. Let him share it with me.

MRS. ARBUTHNOT. But we are disgraced. We rank among the outcasts Gerald is nameless. The sins of the parents should be visited on the children. It is God's law.

HESTER. I was wrong. God's law is only Love.

MRS. ARBUTHNOT. [*Rises, and taking* HESTER *by the hand, goes slowly over to where* GERALD *is lying on the sofa with his head buried in his hands. She touches him and he looks up.*] Gerald, I cannot give you a father, but I have brought you a wife.

GERALD. Mother, I am not worthy either of her or you.

MRS. ARBUTHNOT. So she comes first, you are worthy. And when you are away, Gerald . . . with . . . her—oh, think of me sometimes. Don't forget me. And when you pray, pray for me. We should pray when we are happiest, and you will be happy, Gerald.

HESTER. Oh, you don't think of leaving us?

GERALD. Mother, you won't leave us?

MRS. ARBUTHNOT. I might bring shame upon you!

GERALD. Mother!

MRS. ARBUTHNOT. For a little then: and if you let me, near you always.

HESTER. [*To* MRS. ARBUTHNOT.] Come out with us to the garden.

MRS. ARBUTHNOT. Later on, later on.
[*Exeunt* HESTER *and* GERALD. MRS. ARBUTHNOT *goes towards door* L.C. *Stops at looking-glass over mantelpiece and looks into it. Enter* ALICE R.C.]

ALICE. A gentleman to see you, ma'am.

MRS. ARBUTHNOT. Say I am not at home. Show me the card. [*Takes card from salver and looks at it.*] Say I will not see him.

[LORD ILLINGWORTH *enters*. MRS. ARBUTHNOT *sees him in the glass and starts, but does not turn round. Exit* ALICE.] What can you have to say to me to-day, George Harford? You can have nothing to say to me. You must leave this house.

LORD ILLINGWORTH. Rachel, Gerald knows everything about you and me now, so some arrangement must be come to that will suit us all three. I assure you, he will find in me the most charming and generous of fathers.

MRS. ARBUTHNOT. My son may come in at any moment. I saved you last night. I may not be able to save you again. My son feels my dishonour strongly, terribly strongly. I beg you to go.

LORD ILLINGWORTH. [*Sitting down.*] Last night was excessively unfortunate. That silly Puritan girl making a scene merely because I wanted to kiss her. What harm is there in a kiss?

MRS. ARBUTHNOT. [*Turning round.*] A kiss may ruin a human life, George Harford. *I* know that. *I* know that too well.

LORD ILLINGWORTH. We won't discuss that at present. What is of importance to-day, as yesterday, is still our son. I am extremely fond of him, as you know, and odd though it may seem to you, I admired his conduct last night immensely. He took up the cudgels for that pretty prude with wonderful promptitude. He is just what I should have liked a son of mine to be. Except that no son of mine should ever take the side of the Puritans: that is always an error. Now, what I propose is this.

MRS. ARBUTHNOT. Lord Illingworth, no proposition of yours interests me.

LORD ILLINGWORTH. According to our ridiculous English laws, I can't legitimise Gerald. But I can leave him my property. Illingworth is entailed, of course, but it is a tedious barrack of a place. He can have Ashby, which is much prettier, Harborough, which has the best shooting in the north of England, and the house in St. James Square. What more can a gentleman require in this world?

MRS. ARBUTHNOT. Nothing more, I am quite sure.

LORD ILLINGWORTH. As for a title, a title is really rather a nuisance in these democratic days. As George Harford I had everything I wanted. Now I have merely everything that other people want, which isn't nearly so pleasant. Well, my proposal is this.

MRS. ARBUTHNOT. I told you I was not interested, and I beg you to go.

LORD ILLINGWORTH. The boy is to be with you for six months in the year, and with me for the other six. That is perfectly fair, is it not? You can have whatever allowance you like, and live where you choose. As for your past, no one knows anything about it except myself and Gerald. There is the Puritan, of course, the Puritan in white muslin, but she doesn't count. She couldn't tell the story without explaining that she objected to being kissed, could she? And all the women would think her a fool and the men think her a bore. And you need not be afraid that Gerald won't be my heir. I needn't tell you I have not the slightest intention of marrying.

MRS. ARBUTHNOT. You come too late. My son has no need of you. You are not necessary.

LORD ILLINGWORTH. What do you mean, Rachel?

MRS. ARBUTHNOT. That you are not necessary to Gerald's career. He does not require you.

LORD ILLINGWORTH. I do not understand you.

MRS. ARBUTHNOT. Look into the garden. [LORD ILLINGWORTH *rises and goes towards window.*] You had better not let them see you: you bring unpleasant memories. [LORD ILLINGWORTH *looks out and starts.*] She loves him. They love each other. We are safe from you, and we are going away.

LORD ILLINGWORTH. Where?

MRS. ARBUTHNOT. We will not tell you, and if you find us we will not know you. You seem surprised. What welcome would you get from the girl whose lips you tried to soil, from the boy whose life you have shamed, from the mother whose dishonour comes from you?

LORD ILLINGWORTH. You have grown hard, Rachel.

MRS. ARBUTHNOT. I was too weak once. It is well for me that I have changed.

LORD ILLINGWORTH. I was very young at the time. We men know life too early.

MRS. ARBUTHNOT. And we women know life too late. That is the difference between men and women. [*A pause.*]

LORD ILLINGWORTH. Rachel, I want my son. My money may be of no use to him now. I may be of no use to him, but I want my son. Bring us together, Rachel. You can do it if you choose. [*Sees letter on table.*]

MRS. ARBUTHNOT. There is no room in my boy's life for you. He is not interested in *you*.

LORD ILLINGWORTH. Then why does he write to me?

MRS. ARBUTHNOT. What do you mean?

LORD ILLINGWORTH. What letter is this? [*Takes up letter.*]

MRS. ARBUTHNOT. That—is nothing. Give it to me.

LORD ILLINGWORTH. It is addressed to *me*.

MRS. ARBUTHNOT. You are not to open it. I forbid you to open it.

LORD ILLINGWORTH. And in Gerald's handwriting.

MRS. ARBUTHNOT. It was not to have been sent. It is a letter he wrote to you this morning, before he saw me. But he is sorry now he wrote it, very sorry. You are not to open it. Give it to me.

LORD ILLINGWORTH. It belongs to me. [*Opens it, sits down and reads it slowly.* MRS.

ARBUTHNOT *watches him all the time.*] You have read this letter, I suppose, Rachel?

MRS. ARBUTHNOT. No.

LORD ILLINGWORTH. You know what is in it?

MRS. ARBUTHNOT. Yes!

LORD ILLINGWORTH. I don't admit for a moment that the boy is right in what he says. I don't admit that it is any duty of mine to marry you. I deny it entirely. But to get my son back I am ready—yes, I am ready to marry you, Rachel—and to treat you always with the deference and respect due to my wife. I will marry you as soon as you choose. I give you my word of honour.

MRS. ARBUTHNOT. You made that promise to me once before and broke it.

LORD ILLINGWORTH. I will keep it now. And that will show you that I love my son, at least as much as you love him. For when I marry you, Rachel, there are some ambitions I shall have to surrender. High ambitions, too, if any ambition is high.

MRS. ARBUTHNOT. I decline to marry you, Lord Illingworth.

LORD ILLINGWORTH. Are you serious?

MRS. ARBUTHNOT. Yes.

LORD ILLINGWORTH. Do tell me your reasons. They would interest me enormously.

MRS. ARBUTHNOT. I have already explained them to my son.

LORD ILLINGWORTH. I suppose they were intensely sentimental, weren't they? You women live by your emotions and for them. You have no philosophy of life.

MRS. ARBUTHNOT. You are right. We women live by our emotions and for them. By our passions, and for them, if you will. I have two passions, Lord Illingworth: my love of him, my hate of you. You cannot kill those. They feed each other.

LORD ILLINGWORTH. What sort of love is that which needs to have hate as its brother?

MRS. ARBUTHNOT. It is the sort of love I have for Gerald. Do you think that terrible? Well it is terrible. All love is terrible. All love is a tragedy. I loved you once, Lord Illingworth. Oh, what a tragedy for a woman to have loved you!

LORD ILLINGWORTH. So you really refuse to marry me?

MRS. ARBUTHNOT. Yes.

LORD ILLINGWORTH. Because you hate me?

MRS. ARBUTHNOT. Yes.

LORD ILLINGWORTH. And does my son hate me as you do?

MRS. ARBUTHNOT. No.

LORD ILLINGWORTH. I am glad of that, Rachel.

MRS. ARBUTHNOT. He merely despises you.

LORD ILLINGWORTH. What a pity! What a pity for him, I mean.

MRS. ARBUTHNOT. Don't be deceived, George. Children begin by loving their parents. After a time they judge them. Rarely if ever do they forgive them.

LORD ILLINGWORTH. [*Reads letter over again, very slowly.*] May I ask by what arguments you made the boy who wrote this letter, this beautiful, passionate letter, believe that you should not marry his father, the father of your own child?

MRS. ARBUTHNOT. It was not I who made him see it. It was another.

LORD ILLINGWORTH. What *fin-de-siècle* person?

MRS. ARBUTHNOT. The Puritan, Lord Illingworth. [*A pause.*]

LORD ILLINGWORTH. [*Winces, then rises slowly and goes over to table where his hat and gloves are.* MRS. ARBUTHNOT *is standing close to the table. He picks up one of the gloves, and begins pulling it on.*] There is not much then for me to do here, Rachel?

MRS. ARBUTHNOT. Nothing.

LORD ILLINGWORTH. It is good-bye, is it?

MRS. ARBUTHNOT. For ever, I hope, this time, Lord Illingworth.

LORD ILLINGWORTH. How curious! At this moment you look exactly as you looked the night you left me twenty years ago. You have just the same expression in your mouth. Upon my word, Rachel, no woman ever loved me as you did. Why, you gave yourself to me like a flower, to do anything I liked with. You were the prettiest of playthings, the most fascinating of small romances . . . [*Pulls out watch.*] Quarter to two! Must be strolling back to Hunstanton. Don't suppose I shall see you there again. I'm sorry, I am, really. It's been an amusing experience to have met amongst people of one's own rank, and treated quite seriously too, one's mistress, and one's—

[MRS. ARBUTHNOT *snatches up glove and strikes* LORD ILLINGWORTH *across the face with it.* LORD ILLINGWORTH *starts. He is dazed by the insult of his punishment. Then he controls himself, and goes to window and looks out at his son. Sighs and leaves the room.*]

MRS. ARBUTHNOT. [*Falls sobbing on the sofa.*] He would have said it. He would have said it.

[*Enter* GERALD *and* HESTER *from the garden.*]

GERALD. Well, dear mother. You never came out after all. So we have come in to fetch you. Mother, you have not been crying? [*Kneels down beside her.*]

MRS. ARBUTHNOT. My boy! My boy! My boy! [*Running her fingers through his hair.*]

HESTER. [*Coming over.*] But you have two children now. You'll let me be your daughter?

MRS. ARBUTHNOT. [*Looking up.*] Would you choose me for a mother?

HESTER. You of all women I have ever known.

[*They move towards the door leading into garden with their arms round each other's waists.* GERALD *goes to table* L.C. *for his hat. On turning round he sees* LORD ILLINGWORTH'S *glove lying on the floor, and picks it up.*]

GERALD. Hallo, mother, whose glove is this? You have had a visitor. Who was it?

MRS. ARBUTHNOT. [*Turning round.*] Oh! no one. No one in particular. A man of no importance.

CURTAIN

Made in the USA
Middletown, DE
15 August 2019